THE SWORD & THE SPIRIT

A Negotiation Tale

ANDRÉ BELLO

andrebello.com

Published by: Kiwi Publishing, Inc
Post Office Box 3852
Woodbridge CT 06525
info@kiwipublishing.com
www.kiwipublishing.com

ISBN 0-9777401-0-2

First Edition: May 2006
Printed in the United States
Kiwi Publishing, Inc. Woodbridge CT

· TABLE OF CONTENTS ·

Acknowledgements   5
Foreword by Professor Lawrence Susskind   7
Introduction   9

I. The Sword & the Spirit
    Chapters 1-27   13
    Epilogue   153

II. Negotiation Notes
1.   What Kind of Negotiator Are You?   161
2.   Power, Information and Time   165
3.   Negotiation Tactics   171
4.   Splitting the Pie   177
5.   Expanding the Pie   183
6.   Do You Have an Alternative?   189
7.   Getting a Third Party Involved   191
8.   Negotiating with Difficult People   193
9.   Prepare, Prepare, Prepare   197
10.   Agreement   199

Recommended Reading   201
About the Author   203

· ACKNOWLEDGEMENTS ·

I once listened to an interview with a well-known best-selling author, and I smiled as he described the role his wife played in supporting his writing efforts. It sounded exactly like he was describing my wife Frances. I wondered if having a supportive spouse was an essential part of the formula for writing success. If so... this book is bound for limitless possibilities.

I cannot thank Frances enough for the unconditional love she has given me during this project. From her acceptance of the hours of neglect while I wrote deep into the night, to her merciless critique of each chapter as it was completed. She has helped me endure the growing pains of a first-time writer, and I am truly grateful to have shared this project with her.

My friend Sue Ann is always pushing me. Always challenging me to "go for it". Her belief in me has been incredible and her refusal to accept my complacency challenged me to start writing the first words of this story. She read the first draft of the first chapter and smiled. She said, "You're off to a good start, but..." I knew what that 'but' meant. I would have to re-write. We live in different countries now but I have counted on Sue Ann for her advice throughout this project, and I thank her for placing her faith in me.

My parents, Larry and Shirley, and my sister Francine, have an uncanny confidence in the decisions I make. Even when I am in doubt, they somehow believe that I am doing the right thing. My family's support has always given me the encouragement to pursue my dreams. To my mother-in-law Jackie, I say thanks for taking the time to read my story and provide valuable feedback. There came a point when I re-read this story so many times that little errors or inconsistencies became difficult for me to see. Along came many of my friends, who volunteered their time to review this story. I want to especially thank them for lending me their 'eyes' and helping me bring this book to its final draft. I learnt a saying in Jamaica that goes, *"Good friends better than pocket money!"* and every day I discover how true this is.

I met Professor Lawrence Susskind at the Program on Negotiation at Harvard Law School. Almost a year later, I contacted him to ask if he would review my book and consider writing a foreword. His words of encouragement have greatly motivated me and I am deeply honoured by his contribution to this book.

I have also received some fantastic professional assistance during this project. Anu Lakhan lent me her keen editing skills to help the story flow, and I had the benefit of Anna Kay von Dueszeln's designing skills to help me lay out the book. Anna Kay took on the additional challenge of teaching me how to use Adobe's InDesign so I could bring my personal preferences to the final look. Benjamin Bailey brought his incomparable design skills to the table, and whipped up the unique cover for this book. I was also taught the meaning of the word 'reliable' by my friend Simon duQuesnay who always came to the rescue with his printing expertise. *"Big up Simon!"*

This book is my attempt to spread the negotiation word through simplification and drama. I tried to make the story fast-paced, but complete, and to embed the key principles in a memorable way. The application of these simple principles *can* make a difference in your life and I hope that this book will prompt you to learn more.

ANDRÉ BELLO

• FOREWORD •

The most exciting thing for a teacher is to watch a student take what he or she has learned and use it in new and interesting ways – going far beyond what the teacher imagined was possible. That's what André Bello has done. **The Sword and the Spirit** takes the concepts and techniques taught at the Program on Negotiation (PON) at Harvard Law School and presents them in the form of a fable – a negotiation tale – that will surely help professionals in many fields produce better agreements in more agreeable ways.

We all know by now that new ideas are most easily and most effectively transferred in the context of a story. While theoretical propositions are essential, the connections between theory and practice are enhanced by the rich detail of a case or an example. The way that the kingdom of Cyden deals with the threats posed by its neighbors, the Apanites, illustrates more clearly what we mean by a "mutual gains approach to negotiation" than 100 repetitions of the theory could accomplish on their own. The ability of King Spirus, and his clever son, Anthos, to provide facilitative leadership in a time of crisis, is nothing short of brilliant. And, the importance that historical relationships, unequal power, military might, threats, deception, technology, and information play in the story frame an eminently realistic negotiating situation.

André Bello has worked in a number of different business settings. He has obviously listened very carefully and learned a lot from his colleagues, clients, supervisors and probably almost everyone else he has encountered along the way. There's no other way to explain his unparalleled ability to capture the multi-dimensionality and nuance of the give-and-take of negotiations. He is a storyteller par excellence, but a storyteller on a mission. He wants everyone to be a better negotiator.

The Negotiation Notes accompanying this fable guarantee that no one will miss the most important lessons embedded in the story. Indeed, the ten key ideas presented in Bello's Negotiation Notes parallel the "take aways" we try to hammer home at PON's Executive Training sessions. Bello manages to condense large swatches of the negotiation literature into just a few masterfully written pages.

My hat is off to André Bello. Once you have read **The Sword and the Spirit** you will have been introduced to much of what you need to know to be a better negotiator. All hail King Spirus!

PROFESSOR LAWRENCE SUSSKIND
Program on Negotiation at
Harvard Law School

· INTRODUCTION ·

Read the best books first, or you may not have a chance to read them at all.

– Henry David Thoreau

I hardly ever find the time to read

This sentiment has been expressed to me so many times by busy business professionals that I almost want to believe it. I understand their position well. Time has become one of our most valuable assets and it is becoming harder and harder to hold someone's attention for very long. So, I had a challenge. A mission to deliver a simple methodology for making better deals, to the people who would benefit most from these skills, using a tool that they could enjoy and find the time for. And so "The Sword & the Spirit" was born.

Why negotiation skills? Why should anyone take the time to become a better negotiator? The answer seems obvious... to get more. But master negotiators do not only "get more;" **they give more as well.** This ability to create value that others overlook is what sets these individuals apart. The results: more positive outcomes, creative problem solving, agreements that last, better long-term relationships and in general, success and enrichment in their lives and careers. The best part is... these skills can be learnt. Everyone can be a better negotiator.

Learning to become a better negotiator is easy, and... is difficult. It's easy because the principles are simple, and their application brings immediate benefits to the practitioner. It's difficult because we all develop a natural negotiation style when we are young that is hard to break. We become impatient with the process of change, and go on instinct without enough preparation, often letting emotions get in our way. Teaching negotiation skills goes beyond passing information on to trainees. It actually involves changing people's behavior.

9

This book is a first step towards your behavioral change to becoming a better negotiator. The story was created to be fast-paced and dramatic, simple yet multi-layered, and has countless important negotiation lessons embedded within. The most central of these principles will be discussed at the end of the story, but as you become a more experienced negotiator, you will start to recognise further insights throughout the book. Armed with this new aptitude, all you need is preparation and practice. You will learn to never leave value on the table.

Now go out there and start making better deals!

I.

THE SWORD AND THE SPIRIT

·CHAPTER 1·

I wondered what it would really be like to kill a man.

I leaned a little harder on my knife and felt the blade work its way between two ribs. I expected much less resistance. I did not think I would have to thrust so firmly.

As I stepped back and looked at the handle of my weapon protruding prominently from side of the cow's carcass, I knew I could never do that to another human being. I wiped the sweat from my palms. Even my mock assasination of a dead animal on its way to the butcher's shop was too much for me. I could never kill a man.

But war is about killing men, and war was coming to my land.

I lived in Cyden, and my people were mostly peaceful farmers. Cyden was green and lush, with wide rivers of crystal clear water. Us Cydenites always took great care to live in harmony with our wonderful environment. We produced more than enough food for our own needs, and we were the main source of provisions for the marketplace in the trading city of Hagg.

Cyden was ruled by my father, King Spirus, who was well-loved and respected by his people, and was known throughout the land as a fair and just ruler. Havark was my older brother. He left home when he was just eleven to train as a fighter in the nearby kingdom of Apa. He returned ten years later to mould Cyden's small militia. I, on the other hand, had barely ever been in a fight. I was an inventor and was responsible for developing most of the techniques used to perfect the Cydenites' skill in food production and storage. My mother died while giving birth to me. A small part of me always felt responsible for my father's grief. He never married again.

The kingdom of Apa was situated in the mountains and the Apanites were specialists in the mining and production of metals and alloys. Apa maintained a substantial army of well-trained soldiers and its trade was mostly in weapons and artillery. It was once ruled by King Martol, and during his reign Apa enjoyed a friendly relationship with Cyden. Things had changed since then. Its new ruler, Lord Rukor, was the former general of Apa's army. He came to power by overthrowing Apa's royal family and banishing them from their kingdom. King Martol remained a close friend of Spirus, and after his exile, settled in a small fishing village on the coast.

It was a letter from him to his old friend Spirus that started this story...

·CHAPTER 2·

My dear friend Spirus,

Unfortunately, I am the bearer of dark news. I have been informed by one of my trusted old friends in Apa that Lord Rukor is planning an invasion of your kingdom in forty days. It appears that in times of peace, merchants of war experience economic hardships, as the trade for metals is not as it was.

I am unsure if his intent is to spark a battle that will spread to other kingdoms or if his desire is to occupy your fertile lands, but you can be sure that he is coming with a powerful army that will not be easy to withstand.

I wish I could be of assistance but I am afraid my position does not allow this. I hope that this forewarning will be enough to protect you and your people from Rukor's aggression.

May the Heavenly Father guide you and your people.

Martol

That was the last thing I expected when Father asked me to see him in his chambers that afternoon. I knew that something was amiss when I saw Havark already there, struggling to sit still as he waited for his habitually late brother. The mood in the room was like the weather outside: overcast and gloomy. And as Martol's letter was read I understood why.

Havark was the first to react. He jumped to his feet and shouted, "Has Rukor gone mad or is this a hoax?"

"Martol is not a joking man," said King Spirus. "This is a serious warning... one for which we have little time to prepare. Rukor will probably make his move in about a month's time."

Havark replied, "I believe there is only one way to deal with this threat. Our army is no match for Rukor and his men. We must use the goodwill we have built with our other neighbours to form an alliance against him. Today it is us. Tomorrow he will seek to further expand his kingdom and all in his sight are in peril. We will have to convince the others that it is in their interest to join us."

An alliance? How ironic. It was an alliance that put Rukor on the throne in the first place. It was an alliance that was formed when we were under threat of invasion from the North. That was when King Martol decided to build an alliance of seven kingdoms, including ours, and place his personal guard Rukor as the general to lead us into battle. He got a lot more than he bargained for. Not only did Rukor lead our warriors to victory against the northern invaders, he convinced the best of them to return to Apa with him to overthrow poor Martol. Rukor had acquired a taste for power. It seemed Rukor's appetite had grown, and we were a leg of lamb.

"Anthos, what are your thoughts?" asked Spirus.

What were my thoughts? I had never sat in on a discussion on warfare strategy before. Normally, consultations with my father were about my inventions and ideas to improve our crops. War? Havark was the man. He was actually Rukor's best student. Father sent him to Apa to train with Rukor when he was just a boy. If Havark thought that alliances were the best solution, then alliances were the way forward.

"I think Havark is right," I replied. "I do not see how we could possibly stand a chance against Rukor by ourselves."

As soon as the words came out of my mouth I thought that maybe it wasn't such a good idea. Especially since I could see that

Havark was itching for a fight with Rukor, and one of the things I had learnt is that old masters always hold back a few tricks from their prized prodigies.

Father was looking out the window, probably at the dark clouds that hung over the mountains in the distance. Not too far behind those peaks, the threat that loomed seemed to match them perfectly.

He turned and sighed deeply. "You are both right," he said, "but there are some things that we need to consider. If we start a discussion with other kingdoms, it will not be a secret. We can be sure that Rukor will learn of our plans and accelerate his attack. We will not have enough time to get our forces together if he decides to advance towards us ahead of his schedule."

"You make it sound so hopeless Father," said Havark.

"Sit down, Son."

"Give me ten days and I will take a handful of my best men to assassinate that maniac. He can be the personal bodyguard to the Devil!"

"Sit down Havark!" snapped Spirus. "The body of a snake continues to writhe even after its head has been cut off. Rukor's elimination may create a void that some young hero is anxious to fill. This attack may be fuelled by Rukor's own ambitions or by a greater need that may not disappear with your pre-emptive strike."

"You have been very quiet, Anthos," Spirus observed.

I had lost track of the conversation. Without even realising it, I had started sketching a map of our kingdom on the pages that I always carried. Where would Rukor pass? Would he surround us or attack directly from one side? Could I build some effective traps that would slow him down?

"Are you listening, boy?" asked Spirus.

"Yes, yes, I think you are right, Father. The alliance would probably not be a good idea," I replied quickly.

"I am glad to see that you are paying attention," said Spirus.

I was wise enough not to make any smart remarks.

"The answer to our problem can be found in the City of Hagg," said Spirus, "and you Anthos, are the one to find it."

Havark sprang to his feet again.

"Father, you jest."

I agreed fully with Havark and waited for the punch line.

"I jest not," replied Spirus as he placed his hand in the middle of Havark's chest armour and gently guided him back into the comfort of his cosy deerskin armchair. "We cannot withstand Rukor with the soldiers and armaments we now possess. Anthos, you will journey to Hagg. There will be a guide there to assist you in obtaining the weapons we need. Havark, you will stay here. Recruit all able-bodied men who have the spirit for a fight and begin their training immediately."

What weapons could I find that would make a difference? Was I the best choice to trade at Hagg? I felt that my time would be better spent here, trying to prepare a counterattack against Rukor's force. We would not have the strength to oppose him, new weapons or not.

· CHAPTER 3 ·

Havark was so furious he stormed out without another word. I would wager that he went straight to the river, two swords drawn, making firewood of any vegetation in his way. An hour of this mock battle and he would calm down and then he would call an assembly of his best fighters to give them the news.

I knew better than to disagree with my father on his decision to send me to Hagg. He was the gentlest soul under normal conditions. However, from beneath that steady calm emerged a fire-breathing dragon when any of his own was in peril. If he had a plan, I did not know what it was.

It was time for a calm mind, and there was none calmer than my mentor and teacher, Yoshi. He was my father's closest friend since childhood, and was known by all as "the knowledge-keeper." He spent most of his days in a hidden section of our castle known as "the treasure room." Many people from other lands spoke of a secret room in our castle filled with ancient treasure passed down from my forefathers through the generations.

They were right, but the treasures were not of gold and jewels, but of books and scrolls that had been collected and written over the centuries by my family. For Yoshi, it was his life's mission to read every word in the treasure room, and for him, the value of its contents was far greater than that of any precious metal.

After a series of tunnels and ladders, I approached what appeared to be an empty wall. The entrance to the treasure room was known only to four people, my father, Havark and me, and of course, the keeper of the room, Yoshi. Finding the entrance was difficult. Opening the door was almost impossible... unless you knew how.

Protruding from the wall were four metallic spheres embedded within its stony surface. They were at the height of an average man's shoulder and were separated by the distance of an outstretched arm. There was one sphere that corresponded to each of us who knew the code, and mine was the second from the left. I placed my lips against the cold, shiny surface, and hummed a short tune with four notes. As I completed each note, I could hear a whirring and clunking sound as the bolting mechanisms slid from their locked positions. I was not sure exactly how the lock was constructed, but I knew that there were four bolts, each triggered by a precise vibration, which had to be engaged in a specific sequence. By humming with my lips pressed to the sphere, I was actually using a combination of vibrations in the order required to open the locks. My combination would not work on any of the three other spheres. Each of us had a different tune, known only by its holder, matched to a particular sphere.

I learnt my tune when I was a child and I remembered asking why it was so important that this room be so closely protected. My father said to me, "Information is a valuable resource and will be the key to our people overcoming all adversities that come our way. We must protect our information and share it only when it can be used for the benefit of all." Father's words echoed in my head as a heavy stone panel slid open on my right. It seemed to me that Rukor's attack was certainly 'an adversity' and I wondered if any solutions lay behind these cold stone walls.

"Anthos, my friend," exclaimed Yoshi as the door slid open. "What took you so long?"

Yoshi grinned from ear to ear as he looked up at me over a mountain of paper on the table before him. I could tell that he had heard the news and I suspected he had already counselled Father on his next steps.

"I came as quickly as my skinny legs would bring me," I said. "Do you have a life outside this room, or perhaps a wife hidden in the W-section?"

Yoshi laughed and shook his head. "Nope. No life, but I will file that wife thing in the W-section under 'Wish'."

With that he got up from his chair and pulled me towards him in a tight embrace. I was almost tempted to pick him up off the ground as he stood almost a head shorter than me.

"Good to see you, Anthos. It has been a while," he said. "Is that a receding hairline I'm seeing?"

"Where? Where? It was all there when I woke this morning," I joked.

It was hard to imagine that Yoshi was the same age as my father. Father was in his seventies as was evident in each line of experience carved into his commanding face. I knew Yoshi was his contemporary, but with his full head of jet black hair and smooth olive skin, it was hard to tell. He was slim and short with a big toothy grin always adorning his face. He credited his youthful appearance to three hours of meditation every morning, as well as to eating very tiny portions of food. I put it down to a genetic gift from his Oriental parentage.

"It has been too long," I said, "and I am sorry that it is these unfortunate times that have united us today. What do you think Rukor is up to?"

"Rukor is just behaving in the only way he knows: with violence and aggression. His people are hungry and he is becoming unable to provide. Rest assured, however, that Rukor does not care about the welfare of his people. He remains well-fed, as does his War Council and their friends. However, he cannot risk an uprising from his citizens, and I am guessing that he has rallied them against us, portraying his battle as the noble 'have-nots' against the greedy 'haves'. Rulers like Rukor do not care what you believe in, as long as you believe in something strongly enough so he can divide you against anyone who does not share your views."

"So you think he has the support of his citizens?" I asked.

"The support of the majority who do not know better, yes. They will unite behind him, as his war cry will help them take their minds off their daily struggles."

"Explain to me. Why is Apa seeing such hardships? I have always thought that they were rich in minerals and iron ore."

"They are. However, that iron has only been used for one thing, to create weapons. And if your main products are weapons, you need to have war. I guess there has been a shortage of war these days so Rukor is creating the demand. Since Rukor overthrew King Martol, he has done nothing to expand Apa's trade into other products. However, this is not the first time we have had conflict with Apa, in fact, it was the very same iron ore that was the bone of contention between Spirus and Martol over thirty years ago."

Father and Martol in conflict? I had always known them to be the best of friends. It was Martol who sent us the letter warning of Rukor's attack.

Yoshi explained. "In those days, we were not as developed in agriculture as we are today. Our main product for barter was iron ore that we mined and transported to Hagg once a week to be sold. The Hagglers would measure our goods by pouring the ore into large holes dug in the ground. These were each the equivalent volume of a cartload and they would give us twenty goldtriens for each filled hole.

It was around this time that Martol became King of Apa and he was instrumental in the discovery of iron ore in that kingdom. One week, when our traders went to Hagg to sell our ore, they returned with a note for Spirus from Dowan, who was the chief trader of Hagg. The note said that Martol was about to start selling iron ore in Hagg and that Spirus would have to make a decision about his price of twenty goldtriens per cartload. He suggested that in light of our new competition, we should reduce our price to ten goldtriens. If we did, he would continue to purchase more iron from us than from Martol."

"This is interesting. What did Father do?"

"You know your father. He had a week to make his decision and spent most of that time in here with me trying to find some reference to a similar situation from the past. We could find no such documents. Then one afternoon, just as we completed reviewing our traders' recommendations for our next move, we were approached by General Orland. He was excited to inform the King that he had finally apprehended two thieves who had been pilfering from Cydenite homes in the past two weeks. He had not found any of the stolen items but was sure that his captives were responsible for the crimes as they were both escapees from the King's dungeons having already been convicted for similar crimes. He was seeking the King to get his Majesty's advice on a proposal he was about to make to his two prisoners."

"I remember meeting General Orland when I was younger," I said. "I am sure that his proposal involved an iron bar and a pot of hot coals." I was only half kidding.

"You underestimate our cunning old warrior, Anthos," said Yoshi with his trademark grin. "He was about to make a proposal to his prisoners who he kept apart from each other in different dungeons. He spoke to them separately and offered each suspect two choices: they could confess, or they could remain silent. If one confessed, and the other did not, we would pardon the confessor for his previous crimes and he would go free, but his partner would get ten years in the dungeon. If both remained silent, we would return them to the dungeons to serve the remaining two years for their previous crimes. If, however, they both confessed, we would recommend to the tribunal that they each serve only six years in total for their previous *and* their current crimes. What do you think they did?"

"I am guessing, although they both should have kept quiet, that they both confessed hoping that the other would not," I answered.

"Exactly. There is truly no honour among thieves. They both went back to the dungeon for six years after confessing," said Yoshi.

"That was an interesting story, but I am not sure what it has to do with the iron ore dilemma that Father was in."

"Ahhh, I will explain further. After hearing about the prisoner's dilemma in deciding whether or not to snitch, Spirus realised that he was in exactly the same position. If the prisoners had remained silent, they would have been cooperating with each other, rather than seeking selfish gain. This was the same as his iron ore pricing situation. If Spirus cut his price to ten goldtriens per cartload, he would gain all the sales to Martol's detriment. This would benefit Cyden at Apa's expense. It would be just like the prisoner's confession. This benefit would only last if Apa kept their prices high. If they both cut their prices, they would both suffer and Dowan would benefit from lower prices. However, if they cooperated and kept their prices at twenty goldtriens, they would share the business at a level that was profitable to both kingdoms."

"How was he to know what Martol would do? It would take more than a week for them to be able to meet and discuss their intentions," I wondered aloud.

"Spirus decided that he would demonstrate his intentions by keeping the price at twenty goldtriens for the next trade. By doing this, he would be communicating to Martol his intention to keep the price at a level which he knew would be best for both of them. He instructed our traders to take a simple approach: To indicate our intention to cooperate by keeping the price steady for the first trade, then to match any move Martol made after that. He told them to continue retaliating if Martol persisted in cutting his price, but to stop immediately, and revert to twenty goldtriens if they decided to cooperate. He wanted to make his intentions clear to Martol, so his last instruction was to not vary from this simple pattern."

"How did this plan work out?" I inquired.

"The next week, when we went in at twenty goldtriens per cart-load, Martol came in at ten goldtriens. We took a beating and our traders returned with almost all the iron ore they took to Hagg. The following week we matched their previous price of ten goldtriens, but they had reverted to the twenty. We were able to move all our ore at that low price and recovered from the previous week's disaster. By the third week, we reverted to our original price of twenty goldtriens and they came back with the same price, so we shared the sales fifty-fifty. For many years, we kept our prices consistently matched to theirs, until eventually, we withdrew from the iron ore market because we shifted our attention to agricultural production. This cooperation was the beginning of the mutual trust and friendship between Kings Martol and Spirus, a friendship that continues even to this day. The funny thing is that Dowan developed a strong respect for the two kings, although he had initially tried to entice them to compete against each other to his advantage. He was a Haggler to his core and really appreciated the way the two kings collaborated to their long-term benefit."

"I guess the big problem is that we are not dealing with Martol this time. Rukor is a different type of animal," I added.

"You know what, Anthos? It really does not matter. What it does is put the pressure on *us* to find a solution for *his* problems, with the full understanding that he will not want to cooperate with us. He only thinks in terms of power and force, and will try to grab as much of the pie as he can. It is our challenge to demonstrate to him how we can make the pie bigger, for both of us, and to develop an alternative in the event we fail."

"As usual, Yoshi," I said, "you have brought some clarity to this cloudy affair."

I bid Yoshi farewell, with the comfort that he would be thinking through as complete a defensive plan as humanly possible while I was gone. Hours became minutes, and before I knew it, I was on my way to Hagg in search of the weapons we would need to defend ourselves. I prayed that I could pull it off.

·CHAPTER 4·

"Hey Papa, dinner's ready."

"Papa, come on. Let's eat."

"Pap..."

Jude stopped her mid-sentence. "I heard you, love."

"What's the matter," asked Lia, realising that something weighed heavily on her father's mind.

Jude already knew that he had no appetite for the three potatoes that Lia had prepared for them to share. Three potatoes were more than they usually had for any one meal over the past few months but Lia had been able to exchange one of her favourite amethyst necklaces for nine potatoes. She figured they could have a bit more than usual that night.

"We're going to invade Cyden," said Jude.

"Papa, you are not serious!" said Lia. She sat down on the floor to let her father's statement sink in.

Earlier that day Jude had been called to Lord Rukor's Seven Dragon Chamber. This was not unusual as Rukor often summoned him to ask his opinion on weapon design when his thugs met to play their little war games.

During King Martol's reign, Jude had been his most trusted advisor on metal-refining techniques and machine design. In battle, Apa's soldiers were protected by one of his many creations, an armoured plate lighter and stronger than anyone ever imagined possible. When Rukor overthrew Martol and exiled him from Apa, Jude's head was spared because that head contained knowledge of metal crafting like no other man alive. A head like that was better left attached to its body.

"He wants me to personally oversee the production of three hundred crossbows and ten thousand arrows, and he has given me sixty days to complete them," said Jude.

"So what are you going to do?" asked Lia.

"What do you expect me to do? Perhaps you would prefer a quick execution rather than the death by starvation we are facing now," snapped Jude.

"I'm sorry," he added.

At this point Jude did not know if Rukor was a hero or a villain. Lia and he were not the only ones on the brink of starvation. Apa's traders had been returning from Hagg for months with their inventory of weapons unsold. They had nothing else to trade, and their rocky mountains were not the most willing hosts for edible crops. They were all desperate and they could not eat their swords.

"The Cydenites have always been our friends, but I don't see them rushing to help us now that we are in trouble," said Jude.

"Friendship cannot flow in only one direction. Rukor cut off all relations with King Spirus after he took control. Do you blame Spirus for not rushing to our aid?" asked Lia.

"Right now I don't know what to think. My mind is spinning. How can a man think clearly while he is starving?"

"Martol will know what to do," said Lia. "We must get word to him."

"I'm not sure how Martol can help, but I can have a message sent to him. It should reach him in about six days. At the very least he can warn Spirus of Rukor's intentions."

"Listen Lia, we need to eat," Jude continued.

"I've already prepared some potatoes for us," said Lia.

"I don't mean now. I mean during the difficult days ahead," said Jude. "There's something I need you to do."

Lia waited while her father seemed to take forever to get the words out of his mouth.

"I need you to go to Hagg to sell some crossbows and arrows that I've been hiding."

"Papa, those weapons will likely be sold to..." started Lia.

"Yes, I know, the Cydenites."

·CHAPTER 5·

My ride to Hagg would take about five days so I figured I would have enough time to think the situation through. At the very least, Havark had saddled me up with one of his more obedient stallions to ease my ride. I could just see myself, expert rider that I was, galloping wildly straight past Hagg, all the way to the seaside or wherever else the horse wanted to go. I was thinking about Father's instructions to me. *One hundred crossbows with two thousand arrows.*

Given the size of Rukor's army in comparison to ours, I was not sure it would make a great difference.

There must be something special about those arrows.

Apparently they were crafted by an expert weapon designer so maybe they could do what no other arrow could. Go further, straighter, faster. Maybe Havark was planning an ambush from such a great distance that the response from Rukor's archers would have no effect. Their inferior arrows would fall short of the bull's-eyes they imagined on our chests. The one thing I did know was that Father looked calm and confident as he sent me on this quest, so there was definitely a plan afoot.

I had been riding through the Sirrio Forest for almost three and a half days and wondered how many creatures were staring down at me through the canopy of leaves overhead. I could almost feel those hidden eyes tracking my every move. When I used to run through these woods with Havark as a boy, I was always amazed when he would stop suddenly, then point up to the watchful stare of an owl, strategically perched so he could inspect all who passed by, or the scuttle of a squirrel, just busy finding food with no concern for passers-by. I never saw anything like that unless it was right in front of my face. Havark would also be able to sense how thirsty his horse was. My best attempt was to ask the creature, and since he seemed to nod his head a lot and foam at the mouth, I took it that his response was "yes." I did not blame him. It was more than a day since he had taken his last drink of water from one of the wells that our traders mapped out for me before I left Cyden.

Even with my numbed senses I could still hear the sound of running water in the distance. I could feel the moisture in the air and I noticed a change in the vegetation around me. The tree trunks were getting mossy and damp, and I was starting to ride through some thick undergrowth. My horse trotted through the bushes as if he had been that way a hundred times before. He seemed to know the shortest path to the river's edge, and wasted no time in getting to the cool waters of the Karon River to quench his enormous thirst. I knew better than to ignore the advice of a smart animal so I dismounted and did the same.

Just when I thought I was becoming one with nature and fine-tuning my five, no, six senses, I was deceived by the playful gurgles of the river's flowing waters. I could swear that it sounded like a man's voice calling for help.

Wait... that is a man's voice.

"Help me!" the voice cried from a distance, "I can't swim!"

As I looked down the river in the direction of the cry, the only thing I saw was the churning white water dancing its way past a group of rocks.

"Where are you?" I shouted as I ran down the river's bank with my eyes darting back and forth, scanning the water for any sign of life.

"I can't hold on!" the voice screamed.

There he was, clinging on to a rock, letting go for only a second to wave at me then quickly grabbing at his only salvation. I figured that if I jumped into the water at that point I would be swept right past him, so I decided to run back up the bank, and jump in high enough so I could manoeuvre my way towards him.

"Don't leave me!" he shouted as I turned and ran.

"I'm coming," I answered, as I made my way upstream.

When I got to a point I thought would give me enough distance, I threw off my belt, my dagger and my pouch, kicked off my boots and jumped into the freezing water. It was almost impossible to swim so I just used my arms to alter my direction as I drifted downstream. I had full confidence in my original two-second plan: to make my way to the rock, calm down the unfortunate soul, and guide him to safety as we both drifted to the bank.

That is, until I saw my target rock racing towards me and realised that the only thing I could do was grab the bastard as I sped by, and hope by the grace of God that he did not fully drown as I struggled to drag him to safety. What was I thinking, him drowning? What about me? I was abruptly struck by the understanding that with him clutching wildly to hold on to me, I was probably not going to make it out of this alive.

"Hold on!" I screamed, as I reached out for any piece of his clothing I could grab.

Fortunately, he was so weary that he just wrapped his arms around my neck without much of a struggle as I grasped him by the collar of his tunic and pulled him towards me. As we were both swept down the river, I tried to position our bodies so that our feet would face downstream to absorb the impact of the hidden rocks. I could see that there were calmer waters ahead and after a bit more battering, I would be able to swim to shore and complete my rescue mission. He just held on to me and did not make a sound.

After what seemed like an eternity, I was able to paddle my cargo ashore and drag him out of the water onto the river's grassy bank. I collapsed on the ground, my chest heaving, as I tried to fill my lungs with the air that had been sucked out by my efforts. I lay there with my eyes closed, dizzy with fatigue and wondered how this man ended up stranded out there on a rock in the middle of the river. As my breath slowly returned, I opened my eyes to see how he was faring and was instantly mystified by what I saw... or did not see.

He was gone.

I lay there a little while longer, too tired to think, and starting to question my sanity. Did I just risk my life to rescue an apparition? Where did he go? I wondered if I had dragged him far enough out of the water or if he had been pulled back into the river. But the water here was dead calm. I stood up and waded back into the river, looking for him in the shallow waters. There was no sign of him. I was cold and confused, and had no answers to this mystery.

I walked back up the river's bank, surprised at how far I had drifted downstream, looking for my boots and belt. After walking much further than I had anticipated, I saw my horse standing patiently where I had left him.

That is one well-behaved animal, but where are my things?

I doubled back and stood where I was sure I had jumped into the river. I looked around hopefully in the water and then walked back towards my horse with my eyes darting around on the ground in front of me. As I got closer to my faithful stallion, the entire story suddenly became crystal clear as I saw that my water pouches, provision sacks and blankets were all missing from the back of my horse. They were obviously in the same place as my boots, my dagger, and most importantly, the twenty goldtriens that were in my pouch: In the hands of the thieving criminals who had just robbed me.

·CHAPTER 6·

"I can see why Martol valued your craftsmanship," said Rukor.

He held up one of Jude's two-handed, double-edged swords with a carved bone handle, shimmering with its brass and silver inlays. The sword was perfectly balanced at its hilt. Its blade and tang were made from a single block of iron that had been heated, folded and beaten more than two thousand times to create an edge so sharp it could cut a baby's hair lengthways down its shaft.

"When this is over, you will create one of these beauties for your Lord," Rukor continued.

"I am at your service, your Highness."

Those words struggled past Jude's lips. Rukor's presence in his home made him very nervous and he was very grateful that his uninvited visitor's bodyguards remained outside to keep watch. Rukor was never without his henchmen. However, he did not like to be in their close company as he considered their presence a signal of weakness. He never carried a sword or wore any armour. Instead, he always dressed in a simple white tunic, with black leggings and boots. Jude could not remember ever seeing him in anything else. Jude also wondered how much time his Highness spent every morning keeping his beard so immaculately neat, as it perfectly framed the delicate skin of a face never scarred in battle.

There was no doubt that Rukor was the fiercest fighter that Jude had ever seen, or heard of for that matter, but to look at him one would never have guessed.

His deadly reputation was born when Rukor was just a young man, still fine-tuning his lethal combat skills. After one of his childhood friends was killed in combat, another soldier named Luta was overhead saying that he always suspected that Rukor had been courting his deceased friend's widow, all while the unfortunate gentleman was still alive. This infuriated Rukor, who demanded that King Martol grant his blessings for a duel with Luta to clear his good name and regain his honour. No one knew if Luta's accusations had merit, however, God would reveal the truth by guiding the victor's hand in the encounter.

King Martol hesitated to sanction the duel. He knew that Luta was a veteran soldier and a bully, and that he was highly trained as an expert swordsman and wrestler. On the other hand, he had to consider that warriors prized three virtues above all others: prowess, loyalty and courage, and young Rukor would never be regarded suitable for the company of knights if his honour was in question. Martol eventually decided to allow the duel. He gave the men thirty days to prepare. While Luta relaxed and taunted Rukor on his prospects for victory, Rukor sought the guidance of two visiting masters called the Swordbrothers to prepare him for the fight. He trained day and night, and it is said that he constantly asked God to clear his name and asked others to pray on his behalf.

On the day of the duel, Luta prepared a great banquet in celebration of his forthcoming triumph and asked young Rukor if he had a preference for his burial site. Rukor replied that he indeed had a preference, but would have no use for it for another sixty years. The combatants elected to do battle with cut-and-thrust military blades, and Rukor opted to fight with no armour or shield. This surprised Luta but he did the same. As the two men approached each other in Martol's courtyard, the bloodthirsty crowd murmured in astonishment at Rukor's first move.

Rukor bowed his head and dropped to one knee as Luta approached him. Not able to resist this gift, Luta lifted his sword and aimed a lethal strike at the back of Rukor's head. Just as the sword was an instant from its defenceless target, Rukor swiftly rolled to one side. Some people say that he used some supernatural force to predict his move. Others say he was guided by Luta's shadow in the midday sun. As Luta's sword sank into the dirt where its intended victim had been kneeling moments before, Rukor swept his blade across the back of his attacker's left leg, severing his calf muscles cleanly in two. Luta fell face-first to the ground and Rukor moved with ghostlike speed to thrust the point of his blade into the back of his neck, slicing cleanly through his spinal cord. The wounded warrior lay motionless, with his eyes wide open in disbelief. His paralysed body was removed from the courtyard and it was three days before Luta eventually died from his wounds. No one ever questioned Rukor's honour again.

"How is your Lord's artillery progressing?" asked Rukor as he juggled a brass goblet from hand to hand.

"Everything will be completed way ahead of your requirement, your Highness," said Jude.

"So you can do more."

"Will our powerful army require *more* weapons against the lowly Cydenites? If it is your wish, my Lord, it is my duty."

"No, your Lord's soldiers will be sufficiently armed for the task," said Rukor, his ego unable to admit otherwise.

"You do not agree with this invasion, do you?" Rukor continued.

"My Lord will decide what is best for the future of his people," said Jude.

"Things are very different from the time of Martol's rule," said Rukor. "Those Cydenites get fatter while your countrymen are starving. The time has come to expand our kingdom to its rightful glory. It will be quick. Your Lord will give them the opportunity to surrender to his will," he continued, "but if they do not, their lands will be fertilised with their blood."

Jude thought carefully about his response. He had developed a strong respect for King Spirus and he hoped that the warning letter he had sent to Martol would be enough to save the lives of his people. He knew that Cyden would have no chance against the power of Rukor's army. Their only chance would be to surrender or to seek the aid of other kingdoms. Rukor already knew, however, that they would not have enough time to get outside assistance.

"I do only as my Lord wishes," said Jude.

"But you do not agree," snapped Rukor.

"Do you see us as different?" Rukor continued.

Jude remained silent. He did not know the right answer to that question and he was not prepared to gamble on a guess.

"We are the same, you and I. Just two men trying to excel at their callings," said Rukor.

"This world is divided between those who fight, those who work and those who pray. Just as you work to master your craftsmanship in the instruments of death that you create, I aim to master their use. I have learnt from the great Master Fiore dei Liberi who revealed to me the secrets of unarmed grappling as well as armed and mounted combat. My practices exceed any method found in the written fechtbuchs of Hans Talhoffer. Fiore once said that in his time he met one thousand men who would call themselves Masters, though if their skills were combined you would not have four good students, let alone one true Master. I am that one true Master, and I do battle with God on my side."

"I understand," said Jude.

He was familiar with the fecthbuchs, or fighting manuals, of Talhoffer in particular. As he dreamed up ideas of new weapons, he would often refer to the exquisite illustrations of armed combat in Talhoffer's works. He had no doubt that Rukor knew these manuals by heart, as well as the "Flos Duellatorum" written by Master Fiore. Jude could not help but wonder why Rukor was sharing this with him. He wondered if Rukor was seeking his approval for his actions.

"Your Lord only wants you and Lia to know that as a warrior, his trade is to fight for the survival of his people, and as your Ruler he will lead the battle against the forces that bring suffering and starvation to this land," said Rukor.

"Where is Lia?" Rukor inquired.

Jude felt a bead of sweat trickle down the back of his neck.

"She has gone down to the river to seek berries and possibly snare some fish for us to eat."

"Send her to me when she returns," said Rukor. "Your Lord has some pheasant that needs preparing with her special touch. And she will be permitted to return with one for your enjoyment."

"You are very generous, your Highness," said Jude.

"Just ensure that the armaments are ready in time," said Rukor, as he turned and quickly left Jude's company.

As he left, it became obvious to Jude that Rukor was not seeking *his* approval for his actions. He was just the messenger to sell the nobility of Rukor's offensive to Lia.

·CHAPTER 7·

More than a day had passed since I left the river, but without my water pouches or any food, it felt more like a week. I had hoped to discover another small stream along the way but had no such luck. I did not know if I should laugh or cry at how gullible I had been. But for the serious nature of my journey, I would have considered the whole incident much more lightly, and almost commended my robbers on a highly creative and well-executed plan. I was also very nervous on account of my surroundings, wondering if there were any more watchful eyes tracking my movements through the forest. I imagined that I would look pretty silly riding through the trees wearing no boots, and managed to laugh a little at myself as I looked down at my bare toes peeping out through the stirrups.

This whole affair could have been much worse. I sensed the guidance of God's hand on the day I left Cyden so hurriedly. After I was fully saddled and packed for my ride, Father's courier arrived at the stables with his written instructions, as well as one hundred goldtriens with which I would purchase the crossbows and arrows. My money pouch was not constructed to carry so many coins, so I packed in as many as I could that would still allow the drawstrings to pull closed. After twenty, I wondered if I should get another pouch from Havark, but I figured that he would be out in the fields training his men, so I decided to put the other eighty goldtriens into a waterproof compartment built into the saddle that I normally used to keep my papers and writings. The thieves had no interest in my saddle and I imagined that the twenty goldtriens they discovered in my pouch was far more than they ever expected from a single, unescorted traveller, so they made a quick grab at my supplies and made their escape.

At the time, I contemplated returning home to replenish my stolen coins but I figured that I could not spare the days it would take to ride there and back. I decided to continue on to Hagg and try to complete my task with the eighty goldtriens that I was lucky enough to retain. I was already almost five days into my journey so I knew that I did not have much further to go.

I felt weak and dizzy from the difficulties of the last day's ride without food or water. The night before, I had constructed a make-shift bed of dried leaves, but had not slept very much as I lay shivering from the cold. I awoke before sunrise, took off my tunic and went around wiping the dew that had collected on leaves and grass. After a while it absorbed enough water for me to wring its contents directly into my mouth. I also wrung some water into a small indentation in a smooth rock for my horse to drink from. I did this over and over for as long as there was enough to be wiped, but as the sun's rays beamed through the leaves overhead, the moisture gradually disappeared. I figured it was time to move on.

"Do not worry, my faithful friend," I said to my horse. "Just a little further and you will have all the hay and water that you need."

My stallion was my saviour throughout this ordeal. I was barely holding on, drifting in and out of consciousness as he continued trotting on towards his destination without much guidance from me. While I worried that he might be taking me around in circles, he seemed to head in a specific direction with a knowingness that gave me comfort. I knew that he had brought many of our merchants and traders to Hagg and that the route was almost second nature to him. I only hoped he did not feel as light-headed as I did and that his 'animal instincts' were still intact. I closed my eyes and leaned forward with my hands on the back of his neck, stroking it gently to urge him on, while I imagined myself looking back on this ride as though sitting on a soft cushion, having a goblet of wine and some warm, freshly baked bread stuffed with slices of roasted hog.

I was in a deep sleep, dreaming I was sitting high up in a tree, looking down at the ground at ants that were following each other in lines that created words on the soil. I was thinking in my dream that this was an important message I must remember later. Suddenly, I awoke to the fact that I was no longer bobbing up and down on my horse but instead was falling off his back. I had become so used to the motion of his stride that his stillness threw me off. I hit the ground with a thud, but the surface was fairly soft and my fall was more startling than painful. As I lay on a comfortable bed of hay, I looked up to see my stallion with his head immersed in a water-trough enjoying a well-deserved drink. I quickly joined him, scooping handful after handful into my parched mouth.

"I think you might prefer this," I heard a voice say behind me.

I looked around to see a mountain of a man with a long, red beard holding out a massive water goblet to me.

"My friend," I replied, "I hope you are not a vision because if I am dreaming, I would have preferred a maiden to quench my thirst."

The stranger laughed so loud that he spilled almost half of the goblet's contents as he placed it in my hand.

"It is a good day when even half of your wishes come true. I can only offer you a drink of water," he said with a big beaming grin on his face.

I was gulping down the water so quickly that it hurt my chest. I drank way beyond the amount I needed to douse my craving, almost as if I were stocking up for another day's ride. I had no idea if I had actually made it to Hagg but was glad that my horse got us to a friendly face who could guide us the rest of the way.

"Whew," I said. "Do you think I had enough?"

"You had more than your horse," he answered. "Come with me and we'll get you some food, and I imagine you'll be seeking a cobbler, unless the barefooted look is what the noblemen are *not* wearing this season."

"That is a long story, best told over a hide of wine," I said. "But tell me, what is this place?"

"You are at the merchant stables of Hagg," he answered. "Where are you heading?"

I looked back at my horse in amazement at his navigation skills and I could almost swear that he winked at me as he looked up with a mouthful of hay.

"I am precisely where I need to be, my friend. Now, what were you saying about some food?"

·CHAPTER 8·

"I cannot thank you enough," I said, as I extended my hand to Big Red. For some reason he never told me his name, and I never asked. Big Red just seemed to fit.

"I am at your service, Anthos," he replied. He grabbed my hand with his gigantic paw and pulled me towards his chest in a tight bear hug.

While I wondered how he knew my name, he continued.

"I have heard many great things about you from Cyden's traders and merchants. Although, from their descriptions, I imagined you taller... and much better looking."

At this point, Big Red was looking right into my eyes, trying to give me his most serious expression.

"You should have seen me when I was younger. I would have ridden in here and taken all your woman folk," I replied, at which point Red could hold it in no longer and let out a booming, hearty laugh, interrupted by occasional snorting.

"Younger? You must be half my age," he said. "Seriously though, I hope that you get what you came for."

"I will receive all that is my due," I replied.

I turned and walked away with Red's gift of a big leather pouch slung over my shoulder, but still without any shoes. I had to get those in the marketplace. I could see in the distance, a massive stone wall surrounding Hagg. Dozens of travellers were streaming through a large archway. Almost shoulder-to-shoulder with merchants walking alongside me, I quickly formed pictures in my mind about what they were heading to Hagg to trade. The group just in front of me had to be farmers, as they were discussing the effects of last season's rain on their crops. I wondered why several others were racing ahead of the pack. What did they know that the rest of us did not? Perhaps nothing, as the older, more experienced-looking traders were casually strolling behind me, some smoking tobacco sticks, others engaged in what seemed like idle chatter.

They all seemed familiar with each other, with nods and greetings being exchanged all around. Trying to be inconspicuous was especially difficult since everyone else was wearing some sort of footwear, and stopping twice to remove painful thorns from my soles did not help much. As we walked through the wide entrance, I looked up to examine the stonework of the archway overhead. I had never seen an unsupported arch of this magnitude before, and was curious about its construction. My eyes fell downwards when suddenly the rough and stony pathway underfoot was replaced by the cool, smooth feeling of stepping on a tiled surface. A more soothing sensation I could not remember and my feet quivered with relief.

Before me was an expansive courtyard patterned with large black and white squares. It reminded me of a giant chess board as I watched the merchants bustle across the court, like life-sized pieces in an intense game between the Gods. The large sign erected just inside the entrance made it even more surreal: "PLEASE STEP ON THE BLACK SQUARES ONLY".

This instruction was written in English as well as in five other languages I could not read. As I looked around, I could see that some people were making a great effort to follow the instructions, zigzagging their way towards the market gates, while others walked directly towards their destination, with no consideration for the sign's ordinance. I contemplated my course of action. What could it hurt to follow the rules? I decided to play along. I stepped carefully forward with crisscrossing movements on the black squares only. Was it that the white squares were more difficult to clean, or more likely to wear down from the constant treading of Hagg's visitors? No rule would be decreed without reason so I assumed that there was some logic to it, though unapparent to me.

At the end of the courtyard, I got to a wide flight of steps with numerous small entrances at the top. There were several men wearing bright red tunics ushering the visitors to specific gates.

"Good day," an usher greeted me as I arrived at the top of the steps. "Welcome to Hagg. Would you please walk this way to the green gate?"

He handed me a small green slip of paper and pointed me in the direction of a passageway bordered in green. Right next to it was a similar entrance bordered in red through which merchants were moving quickly. At my gate there was a bit of a queue and I realised that there was a small window in the wall at which everyone ahead of me was stopping. I got closer and saw a sign over the window: "PLEASE PAY FIVE COPPERS TO ENTER".

An entrance fee? I never heard any of our merchants make mention of such a fee. I reached into my pouch and felt around for a handful of small coins. By the time I got to the window, I had picked out five small copper coins and was ready to submit my fee.

"Greetings. May I have your slip please," said the young lady behind the window. She never even looked up at me, and while her voice was pleasant, she had the tone of a well-rehearsed performer.

"You mean this?" I said, waving the green paper, hoping to catch her eye.

"Thank you," she replied, still not looking up and extending her hand towards the window.

I placed the slip in her outstretched palm, together with my coppers, and pulled slightly on one of her fingers as I withdrew my hand.

"Thank you," she said, still with no reaction.

"Next please."

"Five coppers for your thoughts?" I said, with my most charming grin.

"Next please!"

I could almost feel the rustiness in my grin as my face returned to its neutral state.

Cold.

I shuddered from the chill and continued through the entrance into the marketplace.

"I win! I win!" I heard, while my eyes were still adjusting to the bright sunlight outside the passageway. I saw an elderly woman jumping up and down while she circled an equally elderly gentleman who was rolling his eyes in disbelief.

"I told you he would come through the green passage," she said mockingly at him.

"And you are never wrong," he mocked back.

These two were dressed identically in flowing grey robes which matched the long grey hair they both wore in ponytails. I guessed that they were twins, since, with the exception of a neat goatee beard on the gentleman it was difficult to tell them apart.

"Welcome Anthos," said the woman, as she stepped towards me with her arms outstretched.

"Hello," I replied. I kissed her on her cheek as she flung her arms around me.

"Good to see you, my Prince," said the gentleman. He took my hand and shook it forcefully. "Renwick sent us a message that you were on your way."

"Renwick?" I asked. "Who is Renwick?"

"From the stables," he replied.

"Oh, Big Red," I said.

"Big Red?" They looked at each other in puzzlement.

"Never mind," I said, "but how did you know it was me?"

I knew that the answer to that was obvious when they glanced down at my feet.

"My name is Trochos," said the gentleman, "but you can call me Wheel."

"And I am Symfonia," said the lady, "and you can call me Deal."

Wheel and Deal? This is going to be interesting.

"How is King Spirus?" asked Wheel. "It has been years since we last saw him."

"And you," continued Deal. "The last time we saw you was on the day of your christening."

"Father is well," I said, "and as soon as I get some shoes, I will be perfect. Our kingdom, however, is in a great predicament. One I hope you can help us with. Father has sent me with a letter for you. I have it here in my pouch."

"Before we go on, I must ask my lady, what did you win in order to spark such celebration earlier?" I inquired.

They looked at each other and giggled.

"We had a bet on whether you would pass through the green door or the red door," said Wheel.

"And I picked correctly," said Deal.

"It's the first lesson that newbies learn when they come to Hagg," said Wheel.

"The power of the written word," said Deal.

"What do you mean?" I asked.

"Why did you step on only the black squares?" asked Wheel.

"Because the sign said so?" asked Deal.

"Yes," I replied. "I was following the rule."

"Who told you it was a rule?" asked Wheel.

"Because something is written does not mean it is a rule," said Deal.

"Many things are assumed to be legitimate only because they are in writing," said Wheel.

"And many people assume that written words are facts without testing their legitimacy," said Deal.

"So in the marketplace, when you see a price written on an item," said Wheel.

"You might assume that it is a legitimate price," said Deal.

"But it might not be," said Wheel.

"It may have been appointed without reason and may be subject to change," said Deal.

"Some things that are written are in fact legitimate," said Wheel.

"But you cannot be sure," said Deal.

"So we place Spotters at the top of the stairs to examine the courtyard and see how many visitors follow the sign," said Wheel.

"If you follow the sign's instructions by only stepping on the black squares, you are sent to the green door, as it shows that you yield to the power of the written word without question," said Deal.

"And there, you are shown another sign with an entrance fee," said Wheel.

"Which, based on your earlier behaviour…" said Deal.

"We expect you to also follow without question," said Wheel.

"While those who ignore the first sign and step on the white squares are ushered in through the red entrance without paying," said Deal.

"As they have doubts about the legitimacy of the first sign," said Wheel.

"And are likely to question the legitimacy of paying to enter as well," said Deal.

"Legitimacy comes when two parties agree on the same words and their meanings," said Wheel.

"Or in matters of the law," said Deal.

"But in other cases…" said Wheel.

"You should understand that the written word has the power to appear legitimate, and this can sometimes be used to guide your actions to another party's benefit," said Deal.

Hagg was a strange place, and these were two strange people. Nice, but still strange. I would have thought that I would be rewarded for following the rules. Instead I was penalised, and the rule breakers got in without paying. While I was sure that there was a lesson to be learnt in this experience, I was still a little peeved with the folly of this curious experiment.

"Don't be annoyed," said Wheel.

"We are all brought up to follow the rules," said Deal.

"And you should continue to do so," said Wheel.

"But you should question the things that do not make sense to you," said Deal.

"As they may be subject to change," said Wheel.

"And you may have the power to do so," said Deal.

"Today, I would like to announce a new rule," said Wheel.

"Yes, the rule for today is: A prince must have some shoes," said Deal.

·CHAPTER 9·

I handed my father's letter to Wheel as we walked through the narrow corridors of the marketplace. The atmosphere was an overload for the senses, draped with the bright colours of silk fabrics, the smell of flowers and food, and voices raised in too many languages to comprehend. The sky was becoming a brilliant orange hue and Hagg's merchants were either packing up their stalls or lighting paraffin lamps in their tents. As we weaved our way through hustling buyers hunting for last-minute bargains, I gave them the story of why I had no shoes, and how stupid princes can be just as gullible as anyone else. They thought my story was hilarious and suggested I audition for a job as a court jester.

"Is this the place?" asked Wheel, in between his giggles at my misfortune.

"Over there on your right," said Deal.

"Before we go over," said Wheel, as he went down on one knee and started taking off his sandals.

"Excellent idea," said Deal.

I wondered what these two were up to.

"Let us ask you a question Anthos," said Wheel, taking off his second sandal.

"Do you know what a lever does?" asked Deal.

"Of course," I replied. My machine designs were usually combinations of levers and gears.

"The point is," said Wheel.

"That a lever creates great power from a little force," said Deal.

"You are a powerful prince," said Wheel.

"But if you walk into that stall with no shoes," said Deal.

"The merchant will have a lever that will make him more powerful than you in this particular situation," said Wheel.

"In other words, he will have 'leverage' over you," said Deal.

"Put these sandals on," said Wheel.

"And I will take you inside," said Deal.

"While I stay outside to study your father's instructions," said Wheel.

"Come, my dear, and follow my lead," said Deal.

She held on to my hand and pulled me between the open flaps of a bright yellow tent.

"Greetings on this beautiful evening," said Deal to a bushy pair of eyebrows barely visible over a heap of bundled cloth.

"Ahhh, good evening to you, and welcome to Salmaan's Silk Emporium," said the eyebrows that quickly sprung up from behind the mound to reveal their owner's smooth, chubby face.

"And you are Salmaan?" asked Deal.

"No, not at all. Salmaan is a scoundrel. I am his brother Rafeek, and may I add, the only honest one in our family."

It was getting late and I was getting tired, and I hoped that Rafeek was not about to give us his family history.

"But enough of that," said Rafeek. "How may I assist you?"

"We are looking for a tunic for my friend here," said Deal.

A tunic? I thought we were here for boots.

I had no idea what Deal was up to but I imagined that my boots would not be a simple purchase.

"Oh, you have heard of my tunics? Who told you? The secret is out? You know, of course, the secret to Salmaan's everlasting tunics, don't you?"

"Not at all, but if you tell me, it will be our secret," said Deal.

Rafeek looked around suspiciously and whispered, "Hemp. The secret is hemp."

Suddenly it became very clear to me. Rafeek had definitely been smoking too much of the green stuff.

"Ha! Your friend looks at me strangely! He does not know of the many uses of hemp. Would you like to smoke some? Ha ha! All you will get is a headache, my friend."

Rafeek continued, "Look at me. Look at my smooth skin. How do you think I got this way? A dose of hemp-seed oil every day keeps me looking young and beautiful."

He picked up a tunic and thrust it into my hand. "Feel this fabric," he said. "While your tunic gets stiffer and stiffer with each washing, this one gets softer and more comfortable, and is twice as strong. Here, try to rip it."

He held on to one end of the tunic and pulled as he invited me to pull on the other.

"Pull, go on," he shouted. "Ha! You cannot rip this fabric. It is a Salmaan tunic. And its colour will never fade. My friend, you can keep this tunic as a gift for your grandson if you wish, but I guarantee, once you buy this tunic, you will never part with it. So, which colour do you want?"

I was convinced. I was about to point out a really nice blue design, when Deal interrupted. "Can we try some on?"

"Of course, but only at your own risk," said Rafeek, "because he will want to buy every single one he puts on. So I hope you have come with many coins."

Rafeek handed me a bundle of tunics which I carried with me behind a heavily embroidered curtain at the back of the tent. One by one, I tried on the tunics and stepped outside to hear Rafeek comment on how fantastic it looked, while Deal stared on in contemplative silence. I wondered how long this would go on. This seemed like a lot of trouble just to buy some boots. Just earlier that morning I would have given a goldtrien for a drink of water. Later, that very same day, I was going through an elaborate charade to get a price-cut of a few coppers on some boots.

"All right, Anthos, I have seen enough," said Deal, "but we have very little time left. We should be going."

"What? You are leaving? Which tunic do you like? I will give you a special price." Rafeek exclaimed.

"Your tunics are lovely," said Deal. "We will definitely come back here tomorrow."

"Tomorrow? I will not be here tomorrow. You will have to deal with Salmaan. He will rip you off. He will never give you a good deal like I will."

"That is all right. Tomorrow we will have more time," said Deal, "but tell me, what kind of price can you give me on these boots here when I come back?"

"Those boots? How much do you want to pay?"

"I will offer you twenty coppers," said Deal.

"WHAT! Twenty coppers?" exclaimed Rafeek as he stomped his feet in protest. "Those are hemp boots. They will last three generations. You will replace the leather soles a hundred times while the uppers will look like new. Twenty coppers? Those boots are easily worth seventy."

"Well, we will look at them in more detail tomorrow. Good night Rafeek and thank you very much for showing us your goods."

"All right, all right. Give me forty coppers for the boots," said Rafeek.

Deal opened her money pouch and counted out thirty coppers.

"Here you go. If we can agree on thirty coppers, we will take those boots over there right now," said Deal. She pointed to a beautiful pair of black boots that were quite unlike the leather ones that I always wore. I was a bit doubtful about how they would fit.

"ARGGGGG! Are you sure you are not related to Salmaan? Give me those coins!" shouted Rafeek, "and you, give me your cursed foot."

He took my foot and measured it with a piece of string, then went into the back of the tent muttering to himself.

"While you are back there, bring me the blue tunic," said Deal, "and tell me how much you want me to pay for it."

"You will take the tunic?" said Rafeek. He rushed out from the back grinning. Then, he suddenly frowned, "How much do you want to pay?"

"I will pay whatever price you say," said Deal.

Rafeek's smile returned. "This tunic sells for thirty coppers, I am giving it away to you for twenty five."

"That is fair," said Deal.

As I reached into my pouch for the coppers, Deal gently grabbed my wrist and said, "This is a gift from Wheel and me, my Prince."

"Thank you," I said, a bit embarrassed with gratitude.

I took off Wheel's sandals and put on my new boots. They were amazing. So soft that I felt like I was wearing nothing at all.

Rafeek folded my new tunic and handed it to me. "Put this in your pouch, and hold on to it tight. When this blessed woman takes the shirt off your back you will need something to wear."

"Now, now, Rafeek, be kind to an old lady," said Deal.

We started walking out of the tent but there was just one thing that I had to know.

"Do you actually have anything silk in 'Salmaan's Silk Emporium'?" I asked.

"Ha! Silk is garbage. I would never carry that useless fabric in my tent. But nobody knows about hemp. They all want silk. Fools!"

"Give Salmaan my regards," said Deal.

"Ha!" Rafeek scoffed.

These are really very comfortable boots, I thought as we finally walked out of the tent and went looking for Wheel.

·Chapter 10·

"Someone looks very handsome in his new boots," said Deal. Wheel was gone so she suggested that we wait a while for him to return.

"I hope you are not flirting with me. Sometimes, you know, a lady buys a gentleman a gift and it leads to all sorts of romance." I may have lost my charm with the young girls, but mothers and aunties, I could have them making berry treats for me in no time.

"Stop that nonsense," Deal giggled. "Tell me what you observed back there in the tent."

"You mean apart from Rafeek's really bad 'good merchant, bad merchant' routine with the imaginary Salmaan?" I asked, "And your 'leave and come back tomorrow' act?"

"Yes Anthos, those are common little merchant theatrics that both sides easily recognise, and almost out of politeness, never point out in the conversation, but there are three important lessons that I want to identify for you."

Deal continued, "Earlier we spoke to you about power and leverage. These are very important factors in any negotiation and you should understand clearly that the less powerful party can create greater leverage, given the peculiarities of the situation. The powerful shoeless prince would have been at the mercy of the lowly merchant if he was to try trading with him, after sunset, when the merchant was aware he was the only one offering shoes for sale at that hour. So remember... leverage can easily shift during a transaction."

A vision of Rukor's charging army formed in my mind. Would it be possible to find some leverage over his powerful warriors?

"The second thing that you should consider is the amount of information that you want to share with the other party. We did not share our interest in Rafeek's boots until an appropriate moment in our business with him. I do not believe that it is proper to use a false distraction to conceal true intentions as this harbours ill-feelings in the other party, so it was always my intention to purchase the tunic from him. However, some bargainers will try to distract you with a totally unimportant issue and you should be on the lookout for this."

Deal continued, "The curing process of herrings turns them a red colour and creates a distinctive smell. These red herrings were used by escaped prisoners to throw the king's hunting dogs off their trail by confusing the poor hounds in their pursuit. So look out for red herrings thrown in your path. On the other hand, you should decide how you reveal information to the other party. At times it will be important to tell them more details so that an ideal solution can be found."

My father had always placed a high value on the information we kept in our treasure room. He considered it one of Cyden's most valuable possessions. I wondered how much Rukor would reveal to us about his kingdom's hardships, and how much information we would be willing to share with him.

"There are a few other issues that I want to point out, but the last crucial message is the value of time in a negotiation. I saw your impatience growing, Anthos, when we spent so much time trying on different tunics. However, the longer we spent with Rafeek, the more committed he was to making a sale as he had invested a lot of effort in us. Be patient in your dealings. Do not rush your thoughts or accept false deadlines. They are often created only to hurry your decisions and may lead you to accept less than your due."

These were certainly the most complicated boots I had ever purchased. I would have just gone barefoot into the tent and asked the trader for my size. These were really valuable lessons and Deal made them seem so effortless.

"Anthos," said Deal, "you can be sure that Rafeek made a profit on your boots, or else he would not have completed the transaction. The point of a negotiation between willing parties is to put each side in a better position than if no agreement were made. It was his responsibility to get the best possible price for his goods, while mine was to get the lowest possible price. Let me illustrate. You know how a ship uses an anchor to establish its position?"

"Of course," I said.

"My first offer of twenty coppers for your boots had the same effect. It set a guide upon which the price was further discussed. If I had not been as optimistic and had set my anchor at thirty coppers, obviously we would have settled at a higher price. His reaction to my suggestion of twenty coppers was just theatrics, and I knew that I should ignore this flinching. So aim for what you want in a negotiation, not for where you think the deal will settle."

This was great. I had never been exposed to this kind of thinking and my fatigue was temporarily subdued by the excitement of it all. I wished that we could talk longer but I was interrupted by the grasp of a strong hand on my shoulder.

"A fine pair of boots you have there, Anthos," said Wheel appearing from the darkness behind me.

"A finer pair you will not find," said Deal.

"I have made the arrangements as instructed by King Spirus," said Wheel.

"So you should really get some rest," said Deal.

"Let us take you to your room," said Wheel.

"Sleep, my dear, and in the morning you will complete your business," said Deal.

·Chapter 11·

Lia sat on the floor of her room, counting the remaining copper coins from her pouch. She would have just enough for one more night at the inn and might still be able to scrape together enough for a meal later on that evening. She had waited for two days for word of the buyer from Cyden, but up until that moment, nothing.

"What is the delay?" she wondered aloud. "Papa must be starving by now."

She had left Apa with the last of Jude's money and not a morsel of food in the house. An empty pantry was not good company for an empty belly, especially since she knew that Jude was working tirelessly to finish the weapons for Rukor's invasion.

"Hold on, Papa," she whispered to herself. "This will soon be behind us."

"Good evening, Lia. Are you there?"

She heard a familiar voice outside.

"Wheel, is that you?" she asked.

"Good. You are in," said Wheel through the closed door. "I have something for you."

Lia could smell freshly baked bread as she opened the door to her chamber and saw Wheel standing outside with a loaf of bread in one hand and bowl of beans in the other.

"Something from Deal and me," he said. "Are you hungry?"

"Please, come inside," said Lia. She was hungry. Very hungry.

Wheel stepped inside and handed her the meal.

"May I sit here?" Wheel pointed to a small stool.

"Of course. Would you like some of these beans? They smell lovely."

"You would not like to spend time in a small room with a gaseous old man struggling to digest his beans," Wheel replied.

"You are so funny," said Lia.

"Your buyer has arrived today. A little worse for wear, but he is ready to do business," said Wheel.

"Thank you God!" said Lia, "and thank you too, Wheel."

"Lia, your buyer has made no secret that he seeks weapons, and now that I understand the situation a little better, I share your concern about keeping this transaction hidden from the public's view."

"What has he told you?" asked Lia.

"Enough for me to know that you were absolutely right to ask Deal and me to keep your visit here to ourselves. My buyer has no idea who you are, but I will make one suggestion to you."

Lia nodded as she tried to gobble her food in as ladylike a manner as her hunger would permit.

"Reconsider your decision to sell your arrows to him."

"Why?" asked Lia. One hundred goldtriens would have been more than enough for her and Jude to live a half decent life for quite a few years. To leave Hagg with less was not part of her plan.

"Think carefully, my dear," said Wheel. "Your crossbows are the same that have been sold by Rukor's traders for a number of years. Cyden's archers could have got them from anyone. However, those arrows you showed me yesterday have a special design. The arrangement of the feathers in their fletching is unlike any I have ever seen. It is a dead giveaway of your father's craftsmanship. Those arrows will be shot at Rukor's warriors, and will be embedded in their chests. He will recognise them and will know that your father has betrayed him. If he is victorious, the best you can pray for is a swift execution, but I know Rukor, and he will torture your father in his dungeons for years and you will become an object for his pleasure and contempt."

"My God, what am I doing?" cried Lia. "Papa has been blinded by hunger and desperation. He never considered that possibility." She realised that Wheel was right. She could not sell those arrows.

"Do not worry. It is not too late. How were you planning to price the crossbows and arrows?" asked Wheel.

"The crossbows are more valuable than the arrows. I hoped to get seventy goldtriens for one hundred crossbows and thirty goldtriens for two thousand of Papa's long-range arrows," Lia managed to reply while struggling to hold back her tears.

"Long-range! So that is the function of that unusual feather pattern. Brilliant. Tell me Lia, each crossbow is usually sold with a single basic arrow as a start. Is this the case with your crossbows?"

"Yes," said Lia, "but there is only one for each bow."

"Do you have one here that I may see?"

Lia walked over to a chest at the foot of her bed. She opened it, reached inside, and pulled out a single arrow.

"Let us have a look," said Wheel. "Very good. It would be hard to find a more ordinary looking arrow. This one cannot be linked back to its birthplace. So you will be offering one hundred crossbows, each of which will come with one of these ordinary fellows." Wheel waved the arrow at her.

"But he will never buy the crossbows without more arrows. Of what use is one single arrow to any archer?" shouted Lia. She could no longer swallow her food and placed the dishes on the ground next to her bed. She wondered if the deal was slipping away from her.

"Maybe he will, maybe he won't. You will have to close your deal for the crossbows completely before you begin any negotiations for the arrows. Then, in order to prevent their sale, you will have to raise the arrows' price out of his reach.

"How high should I go?" asked Lia.

"Remember, you should use your best efforts to *not* sell your arrows to Cyden, so you will only accept a payment way beyond their worth, no less than sixty goldtriens."

"I am scared, Wheel. If this fails, we will have nothing." Lia sat on the edge of her bed and buried her head in a pillow.

"Do not fear." Wheel put his hand on her back. "Everything will be just fine."

Wheel had full faith in King Spirus' insight and this meeting had gone just as he said it would.

·CHAPTER 12·

These really are very comfortable boots, and this tunic is not bad either.

I had a little extra bounce in my strut, fully geared in my fresh clothes and having a new appreciation for the benefits of a full night's sleep. The house was unusually still and I suspected that my gracious hosts had already left.

What were those two up to now?

I looked up at a life-sized portrait of Wheel and Deal hanging in their dining area. It must have been done when they were in their twenties. I found it interesting that they were wearing robes identical to the ones they wore when we met.

Perhaps the robes are actually the same, made of hemp and purchased from Rafeek's father fifty years ago. Ha!

Out of the corner of my eye I caught the welcome sight of strawberries, bread, and a covered jar that required further investigation. All it took was a dip of my finger and a quick taste test to confirm that the purplish substance in the jar was indeed grape jelly. Under that jar was a neatly folded piece of paper that I assumed were directions for me to meet Wheel's contact. When he returned to meet us the night before, Wheel had confirmed that everything was arranged and his weapons-dealer was expecting me at his chamber in Hagg's Central Merchant's Inn. He instructed me not to ask the innkeeper for information but to follow the directions that he would sketch for me in the morning. This sort of secrecy seemed unlike what I had heard about Hagg, which I always thought of as an open and freely trading marketplace. I guessed that true freedom included the right to keep your transaction private. His map seemed carefully drawn and left no room for error. My plotted path, however, did not seem to follow the shortest route. I was not surprised, as I imagined that for Wheel and Deal, there was no such thing as a short route.

I assumed that Deal was responsible for those strawberries and I reminded myself to find out where they were from. They were sweeter than any we had ever grown in Cyden and I was curious about their origin. I stepped outside the house into what seemed like a hub of trading activity right outside the door.

"Spices and herbs!" I heard from the stall in front of me while the other shouts blended into incomprehensible noise.

I looked back at the house and wondered how it could have been so silent inside. I would never have guessed that all this activity was taking place just outside the door of the quiet solitude that I had enjoyed at breakfast. Could some sort of soundproofing have been engineered into the construction of those walls? Why were there no other houses in the area? In whose room had I slept? My list of questions for the mysterious Wheel and Deal was starting to get longer than my mind could retain.

"Sir, Sir, listen to this!"

A young boy tugged on my sleeve and started dancing as he played a small wooden flute. I waved at him to follow me as I glanced at Wheel's map and made my way down a wide passageway between two rows of tents. The little musician tucked away his flute and ran behind me.

"For two coppers I can play for you all morning if you wish," he grinned as if testing me with his toothless charisma.

Somehow, I did not think I needed to draw attention to myself with a marching minstrel at my side. I also started to notice that

Wheel's route followed the widest paths through the marketplace and I was fairly certain that he was conscious of the number of thieves and pickpockets who lurked among the herds of distracted bargain hunters. There was no need for me to announce my arrival.

"I will pay you one copper to remain silent, one copper for you to get some front teeth, and one more to go get me a bunch of strawberries from as many merchants as you can," I said to him.

If someone was selling strawberries sweeter than those from Cyden, I was determined to find them.

"Sir, Sir, I can get you a whole lot of strawberries. Do you want to see how fast I can run?"

"Show me your speed, young fellow," I replied.

I handed him ten coppers and watched him run off into the crowd. This was what I called a win-win situation. He would either steal my ten coppers and I would never see him again. Not a bad idea. Or he would come back with a sack full of strawberries that I could sample and enjoy. Either way, a certain victory for me.

I tried to picture the person I was about to meet. Up until the night before, my visions of a lethal weapons-merchant left me somewhat tentative, but since he had Wheel's seal of approval, he could not be a complete monger of death.

I will have to be tough, I thought. After all, I had twenty goldtriens less than Father had accounted for the negotiation. If I could get the crossbows for sixty goldtriens, I would certainly be able to get the arrows for twenty.

"I got some, I got some!" yelled my new little friend. I snapped out of my mental mathematics as he ran across my path waving a brown sack wildly in the air.

"I'll get you some more," he shouted out as he ducked between two ladies and disappeared into the crowd again.

It was very likely that my strawberries were being stolen from the fruit stalls of inattentive vendors, but I decided to give Sir Speedy the benefit of the doubt. I kept a tight grip on my shoulder pouch as I made my way through particularly crowded areas. I still had the ghosts of the river robbers on my mind and was not about to fall victim twice in one trip. In the distance I saw the inn, exactly as Wheel had charted. I knew it was not hunger that churned my stomach with every step closer that I took. I slowed my pace and tried to ignore the wetness of my palms.

Father, why did you place such a burden on me?

I still believed that Havark, or one of our more experienced traders would have been better for this task. I could have been much more useful helping to prepare a strategy for our defence.

"Sir, look! Look at how many I got!"

That annoying little voice lifted the thickness in the air.

"Whoa! You filled that sack up to the brim," I said as strawberries spilled onto the ground as he jumped around with the open sack.

"Stand still for a while so I can have a look."

"I filled it up for you, Sir, and look," he said, "two coppers left."

"You did very well." I said. "Did you taste them?"

"Uh huh. All of them are sweeeeeeet," he sang out.

"Let me try," I said. I picked out the biggest, rosiest of the bunch and bit into it pensively.

"You are right. These are very sweet," I stroked his head.

"I think for doing such a good job, you should keep the extra coppers for yourself. Come on, let us see how fast you can run off to buy something nice for your mother."

"Thank you, Sir," he said, and ran off screaming, "I'm rich! I'm rich!"

I stood there at the entrance to the inn looking at him run off and wished for the days when five coppers seemed like all the money in the world. In one hand, I held all the money in *my world,* which was twenty goldtriens short of what it was supposed to be, and in my other hand, a sack of strawberries, sweet, but nowhere near as sugary as my breakfast treat.

·CHAPTER 13·

I made my way through the doorway, turned right and walked past the innkeeper to the third door on my left. One last look at my map confirmed my position. I closed my eyes, breathed in, and made a slight whooshing sound as I exhaled. It was time to go. I popped a strawberry into my mouth, chewed it slowly to pass some time, then knocked on the door.

"Good morning," I said, waiting for a response.

"One moment." came the reply.

A woman's voice.

I felt my shoulders relax as I realised that I must have misunderstood Wheel's instructions. I should have turned *left* and gone three doors down to my *right*.

"Sorry to disturb you, my lady," I said through the door. "I have the wrong room."

The double doors swung open to reveal a petite, dark-haired woman with her head wrapped in a red scarf.

The chambermaid? Did I get my timing wrong and perhaps miss my appointment?

"Are you Anthos?" she asked.

"Are you expecting Anthos?" I inquired.

"Please," she said waving me inside and quickly shutting the doors.

"Did anyone see you come here?" she asked.

"Wheel is the only one who knows where I am," I answered.

"Please sit down so we can complete our business," she said.

This is my weapons-dealer?

"I asked Wheel to keep our dealings private and I'm asking the same of you," she said.

She reached under the bed and pulled out a crossbow and a single arrow.

"This is a sample of my offer. Would you like to see it?" she asked.

I took the weapon from her outstretched hand and examined it carefully with my "expert" eye. I estimated its weight in my hands and held it in position with its stock pressed against my cheek. I hoped that by plucking the string like a musical instrument, I did not give away my ignorance.

"It looks good. How many do you have?" I asked.

"A hundred in total. Wheel has the others stored for me in a safe place, and he'll arrange to have them delivered for you," she said. "It loads very quickly. Would you like to try?"

She offered me the arrow.

"No need. I can see that this mechanism is uncomplicated," I answered.

I did not think it was wise for me to demonstrate my ineptitude and I put the crossbow on the bed in order to avoid any further suggestions.

Should I make the first offer or should I ask for her price?

"Would you like a strawberry?" I asked.

Where did that come from? You are here to do business, Anthos, business.

"No, thank you," she replied. "Are you interested in the cross-bows?"

"They seem fair. What price are you seeking?" I probed.

"Make me a reasonable offer," she said.

I should start my offer at a very low price. I cannot afford to pay more than sixty goldtriens.

"I was thinking of thirty goldtriens," I said.

"Thirty goldtriens? Why don't you just take the crossbows for free?" She picked up the crossbow and put it back beneath the bed.

"Wheel said that you were serious about these crossbows," she said.

"All right, what price were you thinking?" I asked.

"I would not even consider a price less than seventy," she answered.

Seventy? If she is aiming for seventy, surely she can go to fifty.

"Can we agree on fifty then?" I asked.

It was worth a try.

"Did you not hear me? I will only repeat the important part of what I just said... seventy," she said.

This lady means business.

"So should I even venture to offer fifty-five?" I said.

Silence.

I reached into my pouch and started taking out goldtriens one at a time. I was not about to let her know how many I had left.

"… fifty-seven, fifty-eight, fifty-nine, sixty." I needed those remaining twenty goldtriens to have a fair chance of getting the arrows.

"I can offer you sixty. That is my absolute last offer. You have not given me any concessions though I kept raising my offer. I cannot go any higher," I said.

"Give me those coins," she said. She spread them on the bed and began counting them.

"You know," I said, "you are not exactly what I expected when I came here today."

She looked up from counting the coins on the bed.

"What were you expecting?" she asked.

"I do not know, but I did not anticipate such a pretty woman in the trade of arms," I said.

Was that a blush?

"So what is a pretty woman to do? Cook and clean? Will you give me sixty goldtriens for that?" she snapped.

Perhaps it was not a blush after all.

"Are you selling weapons for your husband?" I asked somewhat timidly.

"Are you implying that a woman must only conduct business on her husband's behalf?"

"No, no. It's just…" I stuttered.

"It's just what?" she interrupted.

"Nothing," I said.

"And no. I do not have a husband," she continued.

That was a blush.

"You have some arrows for sale as well?" I thought it best to get back to business.

"You... you want to see the arrows?"

"How many do you have?" I asked. "I am seeking about two thousand."

"Let me show you one and explain its design," she said.

Lia walked slowly to the chest by her bed and removed an arrow. It looked very ordinary to me... slightly longer than the one with the crossbow, but nothing seemed special about it.

"This arrow is constructed to travel almost twice the distance of other arrows," she said. "Look at its shaft."

I took the arrow from her hand and held it up to the sunlight streaming through the small space in the curtains. The shaft was not smooth as I expected but was grooved in a spiral pattern from its tip right down to its feathers. Overall, it seemed lighter than other arrows I had held, but felt weighted at a point one third of its length towards its tip. Its feathers also seemed much larger than those on a normal arrow.

"An arrow that light would normally not be stable in flight but this is hand-crafted, with modifications that allow for extreme distance while not altering its penetrating power," she said.

She continued, "I will tell you right now that the arrow you hold is unlike any in existence today, and will cost you a heavy price."

This is why Father and Havark have sent me here. These arrows are the key to our defence.

"So how much will it cost for the full two thousand?" I asked.

"The price will be eighty goldtriens," she replied.

"That is absolutely ridiculous!" I shouted.

I remembered what Deal had told me previously about anchors and flinching but this price was not an anchor. It was a cannon-ball to the ship's hull, and I certainly did not have to pretend to flinch.

"You are a jester," I said. "Do you really expect me to consider that price?"

"I...I will come down to seventy, but no lower," she almost whispered. She made a small step backwards as she spoke and stumbled on the edge of a rug onto her bed. I stepped forward and leaned over her.

"You are a mad woman." My voice was calm but my body shouted. "If that is the case then I will not accept your price for the crossbows."

"Please," she said. "These are not my arrows. I only represent their owner, and I have been instructed to accept no less than sixty goldtriens for them. This is the value that has been set by the one I represent. There is nothing else that I can do."

Think, Anthos! You cannot leave without these arrows.

"Listen to me," I said. "I have twenty coins left in my pouch. If you cannot move from your price of sixty, then I will have to halve the quantity and accept one thousand, or even seven hundred arrows for twenty goldtriens. I will not leave here empty-handed."

Lia's heart pounded in her ears. She did not expect this offer.

"You do not understand, Anthos," she said. "I cannot sell you any less than the total quantity. It is not my choice. If I do, I will pay with my life."

Truer words were never spoken.

"The one you represent is a tyrant!" I slapped the sack of strawberries off the edge of the bed.

"Those arrows are leaving with me. So there is only one other way to deal with this," I said. "I will get the extra goldtriens and be right back."

I darted towards the door, my hopes crushed like the strawberry that squished under the sole of my day-old boot.

"You," I turned to her, "do not make a move until I return."

·CHAPTER 14·

"Come on, Wheel," I yelled. "Hurry!"

"Run ahead," said Wheel, "I cannot keep up with you."

"Meet me in her room," I said.

I grabbed a wooden post as I swung around a bend and almost crashed into two soldiers standing on the corner. They looked puzzled, as if they were trying to figure out if I was a fleeing bandit, and whether they should give chase or not. I looked back to see if Wheel was anywhere close but he had not yet made the turn. When this was over I would make sure that he and Deal got back twice as many goldtriens as they had lent me, although I suspected that they would not accept my offer. I had no idea what portion of their savings forty goldtriens represented.

"I am sorry," I said to a lady whose basket I knocked to the ground.

"You shouldn't be running through a crowded area like this," she complained. "You could have hurt me."

I stopped and helped her pick up the oranges that were still rolling on the stony ground.

"I am very sorry," I repeated, "but I have an urgent matter to attend to."

Wheel came running up to us.

"Victory is not always for the swift," he chuckled as he ran by.

"I have to go," I left my victim to retrieve the rest of her wayward citrus. "Sorry."

"I will still get there before you," I shouted at Wheel.

I sped past him like he was standing still. It was good to find a light moment in the middle of my anxiety.

I continued running through the crowd, zigzagging my way past curious onlookers. Suddenly, one man's face zoomed into focus from all the others.

I know that face.

As I ran towards him, his eyes met mine and his panicked expression immediately gave his identity away.

"You!" I shouted. "You stole my goldtriens!"

He quickly turned and bolted down a narrow passageway to make his escape. I started chasing him when I heard Wheel's voice behind me.

"Anthos, where are you going?" he yelled.

"That is the thief who robbed me by the river," I yelled back.

"Let him go," said Wheel. "You will never catch him down there. We have more important matters at hand."

A more painful decision I have never made, but Wheel was right. I needed to keep my attention on getting the arrows.

"You are a very lucky man," I said as I watched him disappear around a corner.

"Wheel, meet me there," I said and began running towards the inn.

After two more turns I could finally see its welcome sign over the heads of the multitude. I raced through the entrance and made my way to her room.

I banged on her door.

"It is I," I said. "I am back. Open up."

I heard nothing.

"Open up. I have your money!" I shouted.

More nothing.

"Woman, open this door immediately!"

The most nothing I had ever heard in my life.

"I am coming in," I screamed.

I took about four steps back and ran my shoulder into the middle of the double doors. I heard a loud crack and was not sure if it came from the door or my shoulder. I stepped back and thought that my body could not survive another direct hit, so I jumped at the door with a leaping kick. This time the doors obediently parted to allow my bold entry.

"I have your money," I said to the empty room.

The bed was perfectly made. There were no strawberries strewn on the ground. I was fairly sure that if I peeped under the bed that I would find no hint of either crossbows or arrows. I sat on the bed and bent over with my head between my knees.

But I have your money...

"What manner of madness is this?" a voice screamed at me from the direction of the door.

I looked up to see the outline of a tall, thin figure in the doorway.

"Where is the woman who was in this room?" I asked.

"Your lovers' quarrel is no concern of mine. She is gone and you are here, so you will pay for this door." The figure barked his demands.

"Will this settle it?"

Wheel!

The figure looked back and stepped to his side, out of my view. I jumped up and ran to the doorway to see Wheel's silly grin and the back of the figure returning to his corner of the inn. Wheel stooped down to take a closer look at one of the doors hanging from its hinge.

"It looks like these doors said something to offend you," he said.

"Wheel, be serious. You *must* know where we can find her," I said.

"I only know where she has her goods stored and I imagine that she is on her way there now. By the time we get there, the arrows will be gone," said Wheel, "but let us walk and talk before the inn-keeper decides that one goldtrien is not sufficient compensation for his inconvenience."

Wheel put his hand on the small of my back and guided me down the path towards the exit.

"So are we just going to let her go?" I asked.

"I believe that she has concluded her business with you for today." said Wheel. "Based on what you have told me about your transaction, the issue was one of the absence of a 'zone of possible agreement'."

"The absence of what?" I asked.

"An overlap between the price range that you were willing to pay, and what she was willing to accept," said Wheel.

Damn! Another lecture, I am in deep trouble here.

Generally, I was like a dry sponge ready to absorb the wise teachings of my learned guides, but at that point I was saturated with the despair of my failed undertaking.

"Just relax, Anthos," said Wheel. "Things are seldom as desperate as they seem. Think about what happened this morning.

In the instance of the crossbows, you were willing to pay no more than sixty goldtriens, but your desire was to pay as little as possible and you aimed for thirty. That was a good strategy, and you knew that thirty was too little but you opened low in your bid to set the tone of the price negotiation."

"Go on," I said, looking really hard for the lesson in my misery.

"She opened at seventy goldtriens," said Wheel. "That was higher than you were prepared to pay, so you tested her to see if she would accept an offer that fell within the zone of possible agreement. Your first offer of thirty was probably outside of the lower limits of her required amount, but I am guessing that she would have accepted fifty goldtriens if you had pressured her a little more. The zone would have been between her possible minimum of fifty and your maximum of sixty. You settled on a price at the maximum limit of your zone, and probably could have done better, but a zone existed, so a deal was done."

Wheel and Deal always seem to translate complex situations into such simple components.

"In your negotiation for the arrows, however, that zone of possible agreement did not exist," Wheel continued. "You could not pay more than twenty goldtriens and she could not accept less than sixty. There was no overlap."

"So is it always a lost cause when there is no 'zone'?" I asked.

"Of course not," said Wheel. "Remember that price is only one issue. When there is a stalemate with one issue, there is always the option to introduce other factors that may result in creative ways to solve the problem. This requires that you understand the other party's deeper interests and share some of your own, but this takes time, a luxury that you did not have."

"So you think that with more time, I could have possibly made a deal for the arrows this morning?"

"Maybe, maybe not," said Wheel. "Not every transaction can be negotiated to an agreement. For that to happen, both parties have to feel that they would be in a better position than if no agreement were made. In this case, Lia felt that 'no agreement' was her best option. Unless something was done that made her believe that she would have been better off, she would have made the decision to walk away from the deal, which she did. Clearly the price issue was not the most important to her since she did not wait for your return."

"She seemed scared. She mentioned that her life was in danger," I said.

"Ahhh, I see a protective glint in your eye. I thought Havark was the warrior?" said Wheel.

"Hey, I can hold my own on the battlefield. I might have to bite my opponent, but I would not go down without a nasty fight," I said.

"Ho ho! Let's hope it never comes to that," said Wheel. "Look, we are here. Let's go in and see what Deal has concocted for lunch. I will make all the arrangements to have the crossbows delivered to you in Cyden. They will leave today. You, on the other hand, should leave early tomorrow morning as there is one more person who wants to meet with you this afternoon."

·Chapter 15·

"Please accept my apologies Deal," I said. "It is a shame to not indulge in this feast you have prepared but…"

"Never mind, dear," said Deal. "Wheel will not let it go to waste. Why don't you come with me to the garden and help me pick some strawberries. I'm sure you will have an appetite for those."

"You grew those strawberries?" I asked. "They are the sweetest I have ever tasted. I wondered where they came from."

"Sweets for my sweet," she said. "Come on."

Deal held my hand and led me into a small garden at the back of their little house. It seemed like an oasis in the middle of this confusing place. There was a small pond in the corner of the grounds with a footbridge over it that could barely hold two people. Nothing seemed orderly and there were many types of flowers and plants all mixed together, yet in the middle of this apparent chaos, I was immersed in a soothing sanctuary. Although the combination of colours and patterns of the various flowers seemed random, collectively, they created a beautiful bouquet. We walked over to the pond and stood on the bridge looking into the water at the large golden fish busily swimming around, only pausing occasionally to take what seemed like a gulp of air at the surface.

"So you are off to see Dowan this afternoon?" asked Deal.

"I think he is a long-time friend of Father's," I replied. "I have no idea how he knows I am here."

"Dowan knows everything that happens in Hagg," said Deal, "and probably everything that is happening in the rest of the world as well."

Deal reached into a small sack and threw some pieces of bread into the pond. Several fish rushed to get their share.

"So, should I tell you the secret of my strawberries?" asked Deal.

"I would be highly disappointed, beyond words, if you did not," I said.

"You're looking right at it."

Both Wheel and Deal had the same silly grin, and though I had spent only a short time with them, it was easy for me to recognise when they had something profound to tell me.

"All right, Deal, don't make me guess," I said.

"The fish, Anthos," she said. "The fish provide the magic to the equation."

Suddenly it made sense to me.

"Ahhh! You use the fish droppings to fertilise your strawberry plants."

"You are wiser than you look," she joked.

She was joking. Right?

"The fish droppings make my plants grow faster, my strawberries bigger, and taste sweeter than sugar itself. Did you also notice that my strawberries do not carry the scars of insect attack?" she added.

"You are right," I said. "I did not really notice, but now that you mention it."

I had spent countless hours developing methods to prevent Cyden's crops from being attacked by pests. I tried physical methods like growing certain plants in rooms with sheer fabric walls, as well as various mixtures that I sprayed on the plants to repel the invading insects.

"Any time you have too many similar plants in one area, you provide a haven for insects that feed on those particular crops," she said. "That is why I always keep a variety of plants together in my garden. In this arrangement, no single plant becomes susceptible to attack as there is not enough of any one crop to encourage a proliferation of specialised pests."

"That makes perfect sense," I said. "I have noticed that myself. With my crops, I always plant at least two different species together in the same field. My attempts, however, to rear fish in an artificial pond have all resulted in failure. They do well when there are just a few, but as I add more to the pond, they die after a short while."

"You have two problems," said Deal. "There is not enough air in the water when too many fish are placed in an enclosed space. The second problem is that their droppings eventually have a toxic effect in that artificial environment. If you overcome those setbacks you will eventually be able to succeed in farming your fish."

"You have given me a lot to think about," I said. For a moment, I almost forget about my arrow ordeal.

"I just have enough here to satisfy Wheel and myself, but I wanted to share my experience with you, so you might be able to apply it on a larger scale," said Deal.

"I am very grateful for everything that you and Wheel have done for me," I said. "Although I did not accomplish my goals here in Hagg, your hospitality has been overwhelming."

"Be careful how you measure your accomplishments, Anthos," said Deal. "Your father's faith in you has been well placed."

"I do not know how I am going to explain to him that I have failed. Cyden's survival is at stake," I said.

"Come, my son," said Deal. "Picking some strawberries will help clear your thoughts."

·CHAPTER 16·

How much longer will I have to wait?

I had been sitting on a hard wooden bench next to a metal door at the end of a long, dark corridor. I was waiting to be ushered in to see Dowan. Wheel waited with me for a while but had to leave to arrange for my crossbows to be packed and delivered to Cyden. I was thinking about Deal's garden. It really was quite remarkable. The diversity of flowers it contained served not only to control the impact of pests on her strawberries, but could also indicate the time of day, just like a clock. Certain flowers opened and closed with different natural rhythms synchronised with the movement of the sun. Her dandelions, for example, opened at nine o'clock in the morning and closed at five in the afternoon. Water lilies opened at eleven and closed at two in the afternoon. She combined a dozen different flowers with varying cycles so at any given moment she could estimate the time of day by examining which flowers were open and which were not.

I would love to spend more time with those two. They seem to possess more knowledge than all the books in our treasure room put together.

"Prince Anthos?" said a voice in the doorway.

"Here I am," I said, jumping to my feet.

"Would you please follow me?"

I walked through the doorway into another long corridor that led to a well-lit room at its end. I followed my host down the hall without ever seeing his face and almost bumped into him as he stopped abruptly near the entrance at the end.

"Please go on in," he said as he signalled me inside.

I heard a low, grinding noise as I stepped into a cylindrical room and looked up into a brilliantly clear sky as the roof completed a slow slide out of view. The room's walls were made of bookshelves filled with leather-bound manuscripts and there was a small, round table with a wooden chair in the middle of the floor.

I removed a book at random and opened it to find a handwritten account of what seemed like a dispute settlement between two parties fighting over land.

"Objective standards," said a voice behind me.

I almost dropped the book in surprise. I had not heard anyone come in. I turned around to see a bald, elderly man emerging from a small door that I had not noticed before.

"I'm sorry," I said as I snapped the book shut. "Are these your writings?"

"Yes, Son of Spirus. These are records of every transaction I have ever conducted or witnessed," said the man. "I am Dowan, and it is a pleasure to meet you."

"The privilege is mine," I replied. "What did you mean by 'objective standards'?"

"Would you like to sit? I only have one chair," he offered.

"No thank you," I said.

"Good. I hope you do not mind if I do," said Dowan as he pulled out the chair.

I shook my head and pointed to the chair in approval. He eased into it with a slight grimace and used his hands to pull his legs into position as he sat.

"I have a long history as Hagg's main trader, but now I act as a mediator for the frequent disputes that erupt during trades. This room is where I keep records of all my past dealings. When disputing parties cannot reach an agreement I find that making reference to an unbiased precedent sometimes smoothes the way to a satisfactory solution," said Dowan.

"So you take subjectivity and emotion out of the argument by referring to a standard set in the past," I added.

"It helps," said Dowan. "The challenge is to get people to look beyond their hard and fast positions, and to realise that often, *both* parties can have their core interests satisfied. They just need to take the time to identify each other's interests by asking the right questions and by listening carefully to understand what it is underlying those seemingly hard positions. When negotiators encounter issues on which they cannot agree, using objective standards is a good way to help set some criteria for settlement."

"Let me tell you about a particular case," Dowan continued.

"There were once two neighbours who were both trying to buy the two last ewes available for sale in Hagg's animal market. Both men desperately wanted the sheep and were arrested for fighting in the market while making their bids. What solution would you recommend in such a situation?" asked Dowan.

"In my opinion, the easiest resolution for this problem would be to let each man get one sheep. I think that would be fair," I said.

"Well, I have those two men outside right now. Why don't we go out there and see what we can do," said Dowan. "Come with me."

"What? I thought this was a story?"

"A story without an ending. Let us go outside and create one," said Dowan.

Dowan eased himself slowly up from his chair, using the table to brace his full weight. He walked towards the door and signalled for me to escort him. The door opened into a narrow area directly behind a wide stone table. I was not prepared for the throng of people who stood in the courtyard looking on at the proceedings. Most of them turned their attention away from the two men who stood in separate docks on opposite sides of the quad, to me, who I imagined was unexpected accompaniment for the judge.

"Hear ye! Hear ye!" shouted a crier whose voice I recognised as the same who had led me into Dowan's chamber.

"Announcing the commencement of these proceedings presided by Judge Dowan and his wise counsel, Prince Anthos of Cyden."

Wise counsel? Me? Dowan must have been expecting me as there were two chairs in place.

"Your Honours," said the crier, "before you are Alfred and Uric, both of the village of Littlebury, who have been charged with disrupting the peace in Hagg's marketplace, and whose charges have been dismissed as per the earlier ruling of Judge Dowan. These individuals now stand before you seeking mediation of their claims for the full right to purchase two large, white ewes."

"Very well," said Dowan. "Alfred, please state your case."

"Your Honour," said the man on our left. "I left me house over six days ago with me only mission to buy some female sheeps. Your Highness, I brung all me money in the world to get them sheeps. I can't go back without them. That bastard lives next to me. I told him I was coming here and he followed to try to get the sheeps before me. I should never have told him nothing."

"And you Uric," said Dowan, "what is your story?"

"Me follow him, your Honour?" said the other man. "How could he say that? We both lost our sheeps in the same flood. I was coming here anyway. When he told me he was coming I did not say anything, but I was always planning to come. How could he say that I followed him when I arrove here first. I was just about to get those sheeps when he ran up to me like a madman saying that the sheeps was his."

"So you live next to each other?" asked Dowan.

"Yes, your Honour," they replied.

"Are you not friends?" Dowan inquired further.

"Not anymore!" shouted Alfred.

"Tell me, Alfred, why are those sheep so important to you?" asked Dowan.

"Your Honour," said Alfred. "I have a six-month old baby girl and my wife never produced any milk. We tried to give her cow milk but she vomited every time and got covered with some funny red spots. The same thing happened with goat milk, with a running belly too, your Honour. It's only when somebody said we should try sheep milk that we fixed the problem. Julie takes that milk with no problems. One cup of warm sheep milk every night and she sleeps right through, and the wife even makes her specialty dish with it. It's my favourite! It's a soft cheese she makes in some sort of salty broth. It's good, your Honour. Next time, I'll bring some for you."

"That is bribery!" shouted Uric.

"Settle down," said the crier.

"Now Uric, why do you think you should have these sheep?" asked Dowan.

"Your Honour, let me give you my full story," said Uric. "All year long I had two sheeps in my pasture waiting for me to shear off their wool. Winter coming soon, you know, and I have three little ones. My wife was waiting till the time was right to get some wool to make blankets for the children. When the floods came, all that water wash away my sheeps and leave me with nothing. My children will freeze. One fellow was telling me that I should take one sheep and let Alfred have the next one, but I can't do that. One sheep will never give me enough wool. I need two."

"One sheep will not give me enough milk. *I* need two," shouted Alfred.

"I've heard enough," said Dowan, "this is a simple one. Alfred, you will be the caretaker of the two sheep."

"That's not fair," shouted Uric.

"Be quiet!" shouted Dowan.

I think the whole marketplace went quiet with those words.

"You, Uric, will have full access to the wool of the sheep while they are in Alfred's care. You will share the price of the sheep and the cost of their upkeep. I have put them in Alfred's care as he requires his baby's milk daily, while you will only be able to shear your wool when it is long enough to do so. You will both get exactly what you need and it will cost you half the amount. Now, what happens to your friendship is up to you. Do you agree to these terms?" said Dowan.

"I agree," said Alfred.

"Me too," said Uric.

"Then it is settled, and if either of you complains to me that the other does not honour his side of the arrangement, both of you will be forbidden from trading in Hagg again," said Dowan. "This case is concluded!"

Dowan stood up and walked towards the exit.

"The disputing parties may step down and place their mark of agreement on the decree," said the crier.

I followed Dowan through the door into his reading chamber. He was already seated by the time I entered.

"Anthos, I understand you have a serious situation at hand," he said as I closed the door behind me.

"What are your thoughts on the matter?" I asked.

"I understand Rukor is about to invade your homeland and Spirus sent you here to procure some armaments," said Dowan. "Have you been successful in your quest?"

"Partially so," I said, "but I fear I have not done enough."

"Anthos, a few years ago I had the pleasure of meeting a brilliant French General," said Dowan. "He said something to me that I will always remember. We were speaking about military strategy when he said, *"There are only two forces in the world, the sword and the spirit. In the long run, the sword will always be conquered by the spirit."*

"Those words have stuck with me and I believe they will guide you well in crafting your strategy."

"I will need all the guidance I can find," I said.

"Do not overlook the simple case you have just witnessed," said Dowan. "Behind every party's position, as unreasonable and aggressive as it might seem, are deeper interests that drive their behaviour. These are what you must focus on, as well as your own interests in the matter. These will give you an opportunity to find hidden value and enlarge the pie before you divide it."

"I do not think that Rukor will reveal his interests to us. He seeks power and dominance and we will not have the benefit of your mediation skills," I said.

"Well, let me tell you what I know," said Dowan. "I know that his traders have not been able to sell their weapons in our market. They have been returning to Apa with almost all of their merchandise. There is just no demand for weapons in these days of peace. In addition, he has not been able to purchase enough produce or livestock to satisfy the needs of his people. I suspect that he has used his goldtrien reserves to keep his generals contented. What does this information suggest to you? Think about his interests, not his position to attack you."

"I think he wants to feed his people so they do not start a rebellion to overthrow him, and he needs to find a way to sell his weapons," I replied.

"Deeper, Anthos," said Dowan. "Does he need to sell his weapons, or does he need to earn goldtriens?"

"I guess he needs to earn goldtriens," I said.

"So, there you have two of his interests to think about. I do not know what the solution is, but I am positive that one exists," said Dowan.

"How will I be able to find a solution? Rukor will never come to the table to discuss his problems with us. He is coming to attack us. He will slaughter us while we try to reason with him."

Dowan was already getting up from his chair. He walked towards the doorway, out of the chamber and looked back at me.

"It is time for you to be going. Wheel is waiting outside for you. You should get some rest and depart for Cyden at sunrise tomorrow," he said.

I made my way towards the door and stopped to bid him fare-well.

"Thank you very much for your guidance, Dowan. Both my father and I are eternally grateful," I said.

"Some final words, Anthos," he said. "I agree with you. Rukor is not likely to collaborate with you. Therein lies the challenge. The solution is still there. The responsibility for finding it, how-ever, sits disproportionately on your shoulders."

·CHAPTER 17·

"They are getting ready to leave," said Lia.

She looked out of her window at Rukor's warriors starting to assemble in the square. Some of them were engaged in mock battle, while others sat adjusting their armour. Stable boys were bringing out the horses, all draped with Rukor's crest. They looked so majestic and beautiful that it was hard to picture them covered in the blood of their riders' wounded victims.

"Did Rukor comment on your absence?" asked Jude.

"Not at all," replied Lia. "He did not really pay much attention to me. He would walk into the kitchen from time to time while I prepared his meal but only spoke to his servants. He hardly even looked at me."

"With Rukor, you never know what that means. He might have been observing your behaviour for signs of guilt, or maybe he was just being careful with his words because of his endearment of you," said Jude.

"Papa!" said Lia.

"Oh, don't play innocent," said Jude. "I am well aware of my daughter's keen sense for the subtle."

He continued, "Rukor shares that trait with you and I know he is monitoring our actions. We have to be very careful how we use the money we made from selling the crossbows. I don't know how things will change after Rukor conquers Cyden. Maybe all our burdens will ease a bit."

"Oh Papa! How bad do you think it will be for Cyden? You should have seen the desperation in Anthos' face."

Lia walked over to her father sitting in his favourite armchair and knelt beside him.

"I cried all the way home after running away from my meeting with Anthos. Did I seal the fate of all those people?" she asked.

Jude placed his hand on his daughter's head.

"We did everything we could. I sent the warning letter to Martol. You risked your life to get the crossbows to them. I am not sure those arrows would have helped them anyway. Rukor has enough men and arms to destroy a kingdom three times the size of Cyden. We did the best we could," he said.

"But you did not see his face," cried Lia.

She sprung to her feet and ran to the window.

"Look at them," she said, pointing outside. "They are preparing for a massacre. Rukor's men have been an anxious army with no enemy to fight. When they taste blood on the battlefield, do you think they will stop to take prisoners? This is all sport to them."

Jude went to the window and looked outside. Rukor and his seven generals were riding into the square and his foot-soldiers were starting to assemble. The full militia was about three thousand strong, of which nearly two hundred were mounted knights and the others, infantry. Jude looked at the force before him and reflected on the mere hundred crossbows he had sold the Cydenites. He could see the logic in his daughter's fears. This was going to be an historical mismatch.

Out in the square, Jude could see Rukor ride up onto a stone platform overlooking his men. A loud trumpet blew and the mumbling of his soldiers was silenced.

"Protectors of Apa!" shouted Rukor.

"It has been many moons since you were last called to arms, but your families are now calling for you to come to their aid. Your hungry children, parents and siblings cannot go on much longer without the nourishment they need to stay alive, and you need to be able to provide for them."

The soldiers roared in approval.

"We proud citizens of Apa have made our living for years from our mines, and no one will deny that we produce the finest iron in the land. But who can we sell to? Every week, our traders return from Hagg empty-handed and who has come to our aid? When any kingdom is under threat they come rushing to us for assistance, but today, we are under threat. The threat of starvation. Who has rushed to lend a helping hand? No one."

"They have abandoned us!" shouted a soldier from the crowd.

"You are right," said Rukor. "But your Lord will never abandon you. Your Lord will lead you to victory over those who have deserted you. Victory over the Cydenites!"

"Understand this! Your Lord holds no malice towards the people of Cyden, but that land was put on God's earth for all to enjoy, and you have the right to feed your families."

"We have to eat," a voice from the masses cried.

"And eat you will," Rukor continued. "We are not animals. We will give them the opportunity to surrender. But if they do not, we will take what we need to survive, and kill any man who stands in our way."

"YAYYYYYYYYY!"

Rukor's horse reared up on its hind legs and leaped into the mass of soldiers who quickly parted to make way for him to ride through their centre. His generals and mounted knights followed as the infantry lined up in formation behind them. Lia squeezed her father's hand as the warriors made their way out of the square.

"It is in the hands of the Heavenly Father," said Jude. "We have done our part."

·CHAPTER 18·

"Anthos! Are you awake?"

"Anthos! Come on lazy bones, it is time for a workout."

I forced my eyes open and wondered for a moment where I was. After a few seconds I realised that I was lying in my own comfortable bed, and it was Havark outside my door disturbing the peace.

"Go away, you pest," I managed to croak at him.

"Meet me down by the river after you pretty yourself up," he yelled.

I had ridden into Cyden late the night before and had not slept enough to rid myself of all my fatigue. The ride back from Hagg was much shorter than the ride there, mostly due to Wheel's excellent map-drawing skills. It also helped that I did not have any unfortunate encounters like I did on the journey there. I felt for the necklace and pendant that Deal gave me on the morning that I left. She said it would keep me from harm and I should wear it only until I found someone I felt needed it more than I. I was not quite sure what she meant by that.

I miss those two already.

I dreaded the idea of having to tell Father that I had failed in my mission, although I suspected that he would have already realised such, as the crossbows were delivered a full day before my arrival. I was anxious to hear what Havark would have to say.

He will have to come up with a new plan.

After getting dressed I slipped unnoticed out of the castle to meet Havark. I was curious about what he would have to report about Father's reaction to the arrow deficiency in my delivery. The numerous routes through the passageways in our castle had been etched in my mind since I was a child and I could manoeuvre my way through them with my eyes closed. I entered the garden through a passageway known only to Havark and myself, and made my way down to the river.

"The dead have arisen," he said as he saw me approach. "I thought you would sleep all day."

"You have no idea what I have been through," I said.

"Come on, o weary traveller. Let us see if you still have any use with a sword," said Havark.

He slid his foot under the blade of a sword lying on the ground before him and kicked it into the air towards me. It rotated exactly one quarter of a circle and its handle aligned itself perfectly for me to simply open my fingers and grasp it.

"Which attack do you want?" I said.

"You know it does not matter. Try your best with any approach you wish," he said.

I looked away casually then suddenly thrust my sword at him in a straight line towards his mid-section. He simply turned his body slightly and my blade sped by, missing its target by a finger's width. As I rushed past him with the momentum of my attack he tapped me on the back of my head and laughed.

"One day that little trick will work, but not today... and tomorrow does not look good either," he said.

I spun around with a downward strike to his head that he easily side-stepped. He then ran his forearm into my throat. I could feel him pull back the force of his blow at the last moment before making contact. I took advantage of his restraint to push him away.

"I thought you would have some new moves with those fancy boots you have on," said Havark.

"These are hemp. You do not know what you are missing," I said.

I looked down and started bending over to touch my boots then I suddenly leaped forward and rammed my head into his stomach. While he was still stunned, I grabbed him behind his knees and pulled his legs towards me up off the ground. As he rose into the air I fell forward on top of him and rolled him over into a neck-lock.

"I think I have you at my mercy," I cried.

"Think again," he said.

I could feel the sharp tip of a short dagger pressing between my ribs.

How the hell did he do that?

I released my hold and rolled over onto the grass.

"Do you always have a dagger hidden on you?" I asked.

"Of course not," he said, lying next to me.

"I always have two."

He pulled a short dagger from the outside of his right boot. My brother might be paranoid, but I would definitely want him at my side in any battle.

"Listen, Anthos, that was a really good job you did with those crossbows," he said, in between snickers. "They will work perfectly with our plan."

"What about the arrows?" I asked. "How are you going to deal with that?"

"What arrows?" he asked.

"Stop kidding around, Havark. What are you going to do now that we do not have the arrows?"

"I do not know what you are talking about. Did Yoshi not give you the details of his plan before you left?" asked Havark.

I sat up on the grass.

"Tell me, Havark. What plan?"

"I thought you knew," said Havark. "Before you left, Yoshi spent days in the treasure room researching ancient weaponry that could be recreated to prepare us for Rukor's attack. He came across a weapon used by the Byzantine navy called 'Greek fire' or 'liquid fire', a liquid that would adhere to surfaces and burn so powerfully that water alone could not extinguish its flames. The legend of Greek fire claimed that its ingredients were disclosed by an angel to the first great Christian emperor, Constantine, who cursed, in writing on the Holy Altar of the Church of God, anyone who dared to reveal its secret formula to any other nation. He decreed that they be excommunicated and paraded like a common criminal, whether he be an emperor, patriarch or any other lord or subject."

That is what he was researching when I visited him in the treasure room before I left.

"Yoshi found many writings that speculated on the ingredients of Greek fire and concluded that its main constituents were paraffin, sulphur and quicklime, but there was nothing written about its secret ingredient," Havark continued.

"If I know Yoshi, he discovered what that secret ingredient was," I said.

"Exactly," said Havark. "Yoshi suspected that the secret ingredient was magnesium which easily burns under water. He made several trial mixtures and eventually came up with a fearsome formula."

"You knew all this before I left?" I asked.

"No, but I thought you did," said Havark. "After you left, Father and Yoshi demonstrated the mixture to me. That thing lit up like a burning piece of hell. They told me that the crossbows you were getting were the missing piece of the plan. I was to select one hundred of my best archers who we would place in the fields disguised as farmers. Rukor would pay them no heed as he marched towards Cyden. He would expect them to surrender after he annihilated our knights. As Rukor's men assemble in our fields preparing for their attack, we would pump the Greek fire through the irrigation system for our crops and douse our friends from Apa with some liquid sunshine. My men would then each fire a single lit arrow into Rukor's horde and send them to their fiery demise. No amount of water, sand, or rolling on the ground would prevent the flesh from being scorched off their bones. It is such a great plan. Only Yoshi would think of something so perfect."

"That plan sounds incredible," I said. "So why would Father send me to get arrows in Hagg? He was very specific. He wanted two thousand arrows. Each archer would only require a single arrow for this plan."

"I have no idea. That is a question that you will have to ask Father yourself," said Havark.

·CHAPTER 19·

As the panel to the treasure room slid open, I saw Father and Yoshi both hunched over a sketch that was laid out on the large wooden table in the centre of the room. I knew I would find them in there when my search through the castle turned up empty.

"Anthos! You have returned," said Yoshi. He hopped off his chair to hug me.

"Greetings, Son," said Spirus. "I thought you would still be sleeping."

"Your other son would not permit it," I said.

"Sit, sit! Tell us about your journey," said Yoshi. He ran across the room and dragged a chair in front of me.

"I think I will stand for a while," I said. "I am totally confused. Havark has told me about Greek fire and your plans to use it. What were the arrows all about? I am still not sure if I failed in my quest or if I am missing a piece of this puzzle."

"Take a seat, Anthos," said Spirus. He pulled a chair for himself while Yoshi did the same.

"You executed your mission flawlessly," said Spirus. "Wheel has sent me a full report. By the way, nice boots."

Yoshi burst out laughing.

"I am glad that you see the humour in this. I was panicking all the way on my journey back. I would have been awake all night with worry had I not been so exhausted," I said.

"I am sorry," said Yoshi. "But they really are nice boots."

"So you noble gentlemen had a plan all the time while I was busy chasing ghosts," I said.

"That is not correct," said Spirus, "The planning begins now that you have returned."

"What about the Greek fire?" I asked. "That sounds like a perfect plan to me."

"Greek fire was never meant to be the solution for this problem. All it gives us is a best alternative to a negotiated agreement with Rukor," said Yoshi.

"It augments our leverage, Son. It gives us the power of having an alternative in the event we cannot defer Rukor's assault. It is not my preferred resolution to this dilemma," said Spirus.

"I hope Havark knows that. He is planning to torch everything that even reminds him of Rukor," I said. "So, are we back where we started, with no real solution?"

"Absolutely not," said Spirus, "We have the crossbows we need for our best alternative plan, and Havark has handpicked and trained his best archers to execute it. But most of all, we have you."

"Whatever does that mean?" I was more confused than ever.

"Let me start at the beginning," said Spirus. He stood up from his chair and leaned against the table.

"When I called you and Havark to read Martol's warning letter, I omitted to mention that he also forwarded a message from Jude offering to provide us with some crossbows and arrows," said Spirus.

"Who is Jude?" I asked.

"Yes, of course," said Spirus. "You would not know Jude. Havark met him years ago when he trained under Rukor back before Martol was overthrown. Jude is the mastermind behind Apa's weapons industry and was Martol's close friend and advisor."

"I am surprised Rukor let him live," I said.

"To kill Jude would be to discard a level of craftsmanship that knows no equal. Rukor is not that brainless. At first, Yoshi and I felt that Jude's offer, while noble, was fairly useless as the weapons he offered would have no impact on our cause. However, after Yoshi started to read more about Greek fire, he was confident he could duplicate it and put those crossbows to use."

"So why did you not just send one of our traders to get the crossbows? Why send me?" I asked.

"That was your father's initial intention," added Yoshi, "as we knew we did not need the arrows, but in Jude's letter, he wrote that he would be sending his daughter to sell his merchandise. Your father was immediately concerned. Jude could not have been thinking clearly. Under normal conditions he would have known that those arrows would have given away his identity, but hunger slows down the mind. From the nature of this misjudgement, Jude must have been on the verge of starvation."

"So I sent instructions for Wheel to guide her against selling the arrows," said Spirus.

"This is madness," I said. "I am the son of a madman."

I shook my head in disbelief.

That poor girl. No wonder she looked so scared. She had no right to be involved in the scheming games of Father and his grinning accomplice.

"I still do not understand. Why did you send *me* to Hagg and why did you not just tell me about the arrows?"

"Anthos, do not be angry with your father," said Yoshi. "You are the most creative and resourceful person I have ever known. I suggested to Spirus that you go to Hagg and have the full experience of their culture. Everything in Hagg is centred on negotiations. They are extremely skilled in identifying and creating value between conflicting parties, and there are none more proficient in this fine skill than Wheel and Deal."

"Negotiation skills need to be experienced in order to be absorbed," said Spirus. "I decided to withhold certain details so you could have a practical immersion in their world. I also figured you would be able to pick up some information that could help us to understand the interests behind Rukor's actions. I hope you are not too angry."

I sat in silence. It was difficult to accept that the last few days of my life had been a charade.

"Listen," said Spirus. "Our plan for the Greek fire has severe implications. We will be incinerating thousands of men. Men with families. When a kingdom takes a step in that direction it creates a legacy of hate. The offspring of every dead warrior will grow to hate us, and commit to avenging the deaths of their fathers. We will always have the stain of their blood on our hands."

"In addition," said Yoshi, "our fields will be destroyed, as well as the irrigation system we have taken years to build. We will not have any crops for many seasons. It will be a slow road to recovery for Cyden."

"We will survive and we will destroy Rukor's army," said Spirus, "but it is not our preferred course."

"Your silence is deafening, Anthos," continued Spirus, "but you are the man who can invent options for us. You will be guided by the lessons you have learnt at Hagg and create value that not even Rukor can ignore."

"It is your nature Anthos. It is what you do best," said Yoshi. "You are the only person I know who can think this thing through, and I am sure that your journey to Hagg will spark the solution we need. I am here to help you."

The moment of relief that I felt when Havark told me about Greek fire was gone. Cyden's burden was once again weighing heavily on my shoulders.

·CHAPTER 20·

I am getting old.

I stopped to catch my breath on the spiral stairway up to the highest turret of our castle. It had been years since I had been up there. I used to run away when I was a child and climb up to the top of the tower, imagining that I was my father overlooking all of my territory. I started to reconsider my decision to climb up there again. I did not remember the steps being so steep. In fact, I remember running up those steps with the speed of a deer.

Almost there. Come on old man, get going.

I was anxious to see that view again, to get a real look at what this battle was all about: land. Cyden had lots of it and Apa did not. I had to think about what was at stake for Rukor and to put myself in his boots.

Looking at that view would clear my thoughts, perhaps provide an ember that could ignite a fiery idea.

Fire was on my mind. Greek fire.

A powerful alternative, but one we should keep close to our chests.

Finally I emerged at the top of the tower. The view was as amazing as I remembered. I caught a 'second wind' and ran to the edge.

I could see the wide Turok River meandering through the fields, the enormous Santissimo Mountains to the north, and just about every dwelling in Cyden. I looked again at the mountains and I imagined Rukor's troops making their way over them to claim our soil.

I closed my eyes. I could see Rukor's men riding into our towns, slashing wildly with their swords, setting fire to our homes while mothers and children scampered to safety.

Maybe Father is wrong. Maybe Greek fire is our only alternative.

No! It will not come to that. I will find a way.

I thought back to what Deal told me after buying the boots, about the importance of power, information and time. We would have to build our power, beyond that of the alternative of a fiery response. We would have to slow down his thinking.

He will ride into Cyden and demand our immediate surrender. I will have to give him something to think about, to slow down his thoughts and open his mind to suggestion.

The decision to surrender or not to surrender created a problem. There would be no zone of possible agreement. Father would never surrender, and just like in my negotiations for the arrows, there would be no deal. I needed to introduce other issues, issues that were closely related to *Rukor's* interests, just like Dowan had done with the sheep. I had an idea of what his interests were. He needed a market for his weapons and he needed food for his people. Since Apa had no fertile land on which to grow his own produce, his next best choice was to make a grab for ours. He had no choice really. He did not know any other way.

But what about his weapons? Why was that the only thing he produced? His real resource was iron. Could he possibly earn goldtriens by crafting different products? Perhaps he could. If not, what could he do? His immediate problem was food. Apa had no fertile land, but was there another way?

Although I had some information about Rukor's interests, I had no idea about what was *really* important to him. He would never reveal his weaknesses, and I would have to focus on the right problem. If I selected the wrong issue, it would not create any leverage with him. I had to figure out a way to get him to divulge more information.

Even if I found solutions to these problems, how would I get him to listen?

Suddenly, I remembered my experience with the chequered courtyard as I entered Hagg. It was a clear demonstration of the power of the written word, and when it came to the written word, our treasure room was the authority on history and legends. I would have to leverage that reputation to create a document that would force him to think about his next move.

What if I could convince Rukor that his attack had been prophesied and documented in our treasure room, and that this prophecy predicted he would be a hero to his people without striking a single blow? His ego would not be able to resist that possibility.

This idea would give us some time while he considered the implications of the prophecy. We would have to pretend that we always knew he was coming and were waiting for him to arrive. His deadline for our decision on an immediate surrender would be stretched. We would have to use that extra time wisely.

We can slow down the speed of the negotiation to our benefit. But how can we use that extra time? How can I show Rukor that it is not in his interest to attack us?

I knew that I had to solve his problems for him. I had to find a way for him to sell his weapons, or a way for him to feed his people. We could not offer our charity. It was too late for that. He would feel too humiliated in front of his people to accept.

I wondered how I could help him sell weapons when the proficient traders at Hagg could not. It would be impossible. But were weapons Rukor's actual resource, or was it something else? What was it that Rukor really had to offer?

He really is in the business of iron and has the skill to produce iron products.

I knew I would have to think about this some more. I looked out again at the Turok River. In the distance I could see some fishermen in a boat pulling up their nets.

Does that river not originate in the mountains of Apa?

I was sure that it did. Its banks would not be as wide as in Cyden but I was positive that it ran through Apa as a fast-moving stream.

There would not be enough fish in its streams to be of much use. Unless...

A vision flashed into my mind.

Deal, you brilliant woman! This is perfect. It would not only solve Rukor's problems, but will be a great benefit to us as well. I have to tell Yoshi.

Those steps were a lot friendlier on the way down, but still, I could not get off that tower fast enough. There would be a whole lot to prepare.

·CHAPTER 21·

"General, all the men have changed their clothing."

"Do they all have their crossbows?" asked Havark.

"They are getting them now. Should I assemble them for you?"

"It is time," Havark replied.

The men started coming together in a clearing by the river that was like a second home to all of them. Each had a favourite spot - under a tree, on a rock or by the bridge - which he would frequent as they rested during the rigorous drills and simulations that they practised every day. Havark threw everything at them, from grappling and wrestling, to eastern martial arts, as well as weapons training. His weapon of choice was the two-handed broadsword but all his men knew to expect a sneaky dagger attack at all times. Each of Havark's men was an expert fighter, easily capable of dispatching five or six attackers at a time, but the sheer numbers of Rukor's warriors would completely overwhelm them. That is, if they were to engage in conventional warfare on the battlefield. Yoshi had seen to it that they would not have to face that possibility.

"Look at you, said Havark to his troops. "Where are my fierce warriors? All I see before me is a bunch of farmers."

The men laughed as they looked at each other. To anyone who knew what these men were capable of, the joke was obvious.

"My brothers," said Havark. "Today you conceal your strength under the simple clothes of farmers in order to outwit your enemy and deal him a terminal blow. You have all been training tirelessly with your new crossbows. Does anyone know why?"

"Forgive me, General," said a young soldier in the front. "I've been training as hard as anyone else, but I'm not sure how one hundred crossbows will help us against thousands of Rukor's men."

An older soldier clouted him on the back of his head.

"You should have faith in your General's plan," he scolded.

"No, no," said Havark, "he has a right to ask. Today it will become clear to you. You will be introduced to a weapon that once inspired fear in the souls of its possessor's enemies. A weapon that has been kept secret for many years. That is, of course, until our Yoshi got his hands on it."

Laughter spread among the men.

"I will save my words in describing this weapon to you. I will let you witness its potent power with your own eyes," said Havark.

He walked over to a wooden pail behind him and reached down beside it to pick up a chain with a small iron ball attached to its end. He then faced his men and started swinging the ball in a circle above his head.

"This, my brothers, is *not* the weapon," he said.

"That's a relief!" shouted a voice from the back.

More laughter. Havark knew that it was important to maintain a good sense of humour in order to keep his men relaxed, even in the face of the serious nature of their undertaking. He stopped swinging the ball and dipped it into the wooden pail. One of his senior soldiers stepped up to him with a torch and ignited the metal ball. A murmur spread among the men as Havark started swinging the fiery ball in a circular motion over his head again.

"We are getting warmer," he said.

He made his way through the seated soldiers, and across to the bridge, still creating a flaming halo around his head with the spinning ball and chain. Everyone jumped to their feet and lined the river's bank so they could see what came next.

"Behold!" he shouted, as he stood in the middle of the bridge and slowly lowered the burning sphere into the water by its chain. He kept the ball submerged while his men speculated about what they were supposed to be witnessing. When he was satisfied that he had infused enough drama into the scene, Havark slowly pulled the ball back out of the water. And it still burned as fiercely as before.

The men cheered loudly.

"This is Greek fire, my friends, and we shall be applying a fresh coat to each and every one of our Apanite guests as they stand preparing to attack us in our fields," said Havark.

He continued to address his men from the bridge.

"You men will go to the outer edges of our fields and cover your crossbows with leaves. Ensure that they are well hidden. Each of you will have an arrow with its tip dipped in Greek fire, and flint stones with which to ignite it. You will also have sickles and scythes. Remember, you are all farmers, so you will be harvesting your crops as Rukor's troops ride by."

"I don't know if I'll be able to resist pulling one of those savages off his horse as he rides by," mumbled one soldier to another beside him.

An ordinary man might have missed his muttering but Havark's senses were unnaturally sharp.

"Listen to me carefully!" shouted Havark, glaring in the direction of the voice. "Under no circumstance is anyone to act until they get my signal. That signal is a flaming arrow shot into the air from the castle. Do you understand me?"

"Yes, General," shouted the men.

"Good. Yoshi has prepared a cauldron of Greek fire and has fed it directly into the irrigation system for our crops. My signal will not be sent until the system has been engaged and Rukor's men have been sprinkled with our blessings. Only then will I signal you to light your arrows and shoot your flames into the fields."

"Yes, General!"

"I want to make one thing perfectly clear. We are prepared to negotiate with Rukor as our first option. It is our intention to avoid warfare. Our plan to use Greek fire is an absolute last resort. Do not fire unless you see my signal," screamed Havark. "If you do not see my signal, it means that the negotiations have been successful and Rukor has decided to retreat. Allow him and his men to leave peacefully."

"As you order General."

"I repeat, Greek fire is our last resort, not our first option. Is that clear?"

"Yes, General!"

Suddenly, Havark realised that all eyes had shifted away from him and were focused on some distraction on the distant side of the river.

"Look, Prince Havark," shouted a soldier on the bridge. "Here comes a rider."

A horse with its rider raced towards the bridge from the side of the river opposite to where the men were assembled. He approached the bridge, leaped off his horse and ran down the bridge towards Havark.

"They're coming! They're coming!" he yelled.

The rider's face was pale with panic. Havark imagined that he had seen many more men than he was expecting. He held the rider by both shoulders as if to comfort him.

"How much time do you think we have?" asked Havark.

"Three, maybe four hours," the rider replied, still trying to catch his breath.

"That is all the time we need."

·CHAPTER 22·

"You need to relax, Anthos," said Spirus.

"I am perfectly calm," I replied.

"Somehow, the furrows you are leaving in the floor from pacing back and forth tell a different story," said Spirus.

"I am just trying to figure out if there is anything that we have overlooked," I said.

Father and I were in his chamber where this entire thing had all started for me. We were waiting for the final word of Rukor's arrival. Yoshi and Havark had everything in place for our Greek fire alternative, while Father and I had worked tirelessly to compose the dialogue and supporting documents for our pending discussion with Rukor.

"Son, as you know, there are many sources of power in a negotiation. Rukor comes here with physical power, but we have the power of information, moral authority and expertise, all backed up with the power to defeat him in battle if we are forced to. We are in an excellent position and have completed the most important task for this encounter. We have prepared for all possibilities. He is only prepared for a fight. We will bridge his lack of preparation to negotiate with our information. The creative options that you have developed truly offer mutual benefits that will be difficult for Rukor to overlook."

"We have come far since we first received Martol's warning," I said.

"*You* have come far, Anthos," said Spirus.

He walked up to me and patted me gently on my stomach.

"I know how you feel," he said, "in the pit of your gut. That feeling is just an indicator of the day's importance. As confident as Rukor is, he feels the same. The difference is, that we are ready."

"Two days in Hagg really taught me a tremendous amount," I said.

"That learning would have been wasted if you did not apply it," said Spirus, "and you have applied it well."

As we hugged each other we were interrupted by a knock on the door.

"Begging your pardon, your Highness."

One of Havark's young warriors peeped through the open door.

"I've come to report that the archers are positioned in the fields, ready and waiting. The rest of the men are in the courtyard to provide your protection," he said.

"What about the women and children?" asked Spirus.

"We split them up, your Highness," he said. "We brought as many as we could into the castle, and we spread the others in the sunken caves in the Losdon forest. We sent them there with enough food and water to last about three weeks."

"Very good," said Father.

The young warrior smiled with pride.

"All the men have volunteered to fight, your Highness," he continued, "even the real farmers. Prince Havark gave them weapons and sent some to guard the women. All the others are waiting in the courtyard."

Just then, a familiar faced appeared at the door.

"Yoshi! Come on in," I greeted him.

"No time, Anthos," he said. "Rukor is here."

·CHAPTER 23·

"Cyden is just over that ridge, my Lord."

Rukor looked over at Oleg, one of his most trusted Generals.

"Point me to a spot where I can get a good view," said Rukor.

"Over there, by the tree. From there you will be able to see all of Cyden," said Oleg.

"Accompany your Lord," commanded Rukor.

He dug his heels into his horse's sides and raced towards the tree. Oleg followed. Rukor sat in his saddle, surveying the horizon with a calculating eye. King Spirus' castle was the first thing to catch his attention, standing majestically above the smaller surrounding houses scattered among Cyden's fertile fields. He shook his head at how badly structured Cyden was to withstand an attack. No fortifying walls. No moat. The castle was totally unprotected. This would have to change once he assumed control.

"Start getting the men into formation," said Rukor.

"Right away, my Lord," said Oleg.

"Oleg, at your Lord's command, the men will stop in the fields just in front of Spirus' castle in preparation for their advance. You will accompany your Lord to demand Cyden's surrender. By now Spirus must know we are on our way. He must also know that he has no alternative but to surrender. His army is no match for ours."

"I will give the order, my Lord."

Oleg rode down the slope shouting his orders to the other generals.

Rukor looked over the fields and had no idea what kind of crops they were. He also did not know how to plant crops, harvest them, anything... he did not know *anything* about farming, and he did not think that anyone in Apa knew anything either. Just then, his thoughts were interrupted by Oleg's return.

"My Lord! The men are reporting that there are farmers in the fields!"

"Are they offering resistance?" asked Rukor.

"No, my Lord. They are running. They were in the middle of harvesting their crops," said Oleg.

"They are of no consequence," said Rukor. "They will provide the labour we need when this is over. Instruct our men to ignore them and to continue on towards the castle."

"Yes, my Lord," Oleg rode back down to meet the soldiers, shouting out his commands.

Rukor knew that this invasion was all about his ability to lead his people, and hungry people were hard to lead. Hungry soldiers needed little encouragement to overthrow their generals. He had full confidence in his closest generals and always ensured that they shared in his spoils. The masses, however, were another thing. For some time, Apa's citizens had been nursing hungry bellies, but Rukor was forced to make a move only when that hunger started to spread to his warriors. Food was an essential element in his formula for power, and he knew that Cyden was an ample source of provisions towards his cause. He cursed the wretched, barren land of Apa. Its stony ground gave up precious iron ore but not a single ear of corn. Hungry men could not eat iron ore.

He pulled on his reins and started down the hill to join his men. It had been a long time since he had been engaged in full battle. He wondered about Havark. There had been no soldier under his command who had ever demonstrated Havark's natural fighting skills.

Rukor planned to seek him out on the battlefield and deliver a final lesson to his former student.

A lesson in the graceful art of death.

·CHAPTER 24·

I looked around at the faces of our soldiers in the courtyard. They seemed so composed. They must have had full confidence in their brothers out in the fields. Father looked the same. Was I the odd man out? This plan was my doing and I was holding myself fully accountable for its success.

"Here he comes," said Spirus.

I watched our men part to allow two riders to enter the courtyard. One was heavily armoured and rode with his sword in hand, while the other wore a simple tunic and a look of self-assurance on his face. There was no doubt in my mind which one was Rukor.

"King Spirus!" shouted Rukor as he continued to ride towards us.

"Today is not a good day for you," he continued.

"Every day is a good day for me, Rukor," said Spirus.

By this time, Rukor and his companion had stopped an arm's length in front of Father. I knew that Havark was watching from the tower and must have been shaking with rage.

"Welcome to Cyden," said Spirus. "I hope that your ride was not too tiresome."

"Do not fool around with me, old man!" shouted Rukor. "You know why I am here."

Forget Havark! I am going to murder this creature myself.

Father did not flinch.

"I only know that you have come a long way with a large number of men who are now assembled in front of my castle. Tell me Rukor, why are you here?"

"I am a merciful man. I will give you no less of an opportunity to save your life than I did your friend Martol. Surrender to me now and I will spare the lives of you and your family. Do not hesitate. The consequences are dire," said Rukor.

"I am afraid that neither of those options appears attractive to me," said Spirus. "I neither accept them nor reject them at this time. What I would like to know is this: how will attacking Cyden address your problems?"

"You are playing with me Spirus. You have just run out of time."

Rukor pulled fiercely on his reins and turned to ride out.

"Rukor! Cyden is not your problem. We are not the enemy destroying your kingdom," said Spirus. "In fact, we have been waiting for you."

Rukor stopped and turned around.

"Waiting for me?" he asked. "The only one here who should be waiting for me is your son, waiting for me to continue slapping him around like when he was a boy."

Somehow, someone slapping Havark around was not something that I could easily imagine.

"Rukor, we have scrolls in our treasure room that have prophesied this very day and we have been prepared for your arrival. Look around you. Do you see fear? This day brings opportunity, but only if you care to embrace it," said Spirus.

"Of what nonsense do you speak? Prophecy? Do you think I am a simpleton?" Rukor snarled.

"I am only describing what others before me have written," said Spirus. "Perhaps you would prefer to read it yourself?"

That was my cue to step forward and present the "ancient" scroll to Rukor. I had spent many hours trying to get the wording just right while Yoshi had worked his magic to make the papyrus on which it was written appear hundreds of years old. It needed to sound like the unbiased wisdom of some ancient sage and not crafted by Yoshi and me over the past few days. The lesson of the power of the written word was not wasted on me. Neither was insight from Dowan on the use of objective third-party information.

"Lord Rukor! Lord Rukor!" cried a man racing into the courtyard on horseback.

"Something is happening in the fields!"

The ever-reliable Yoshi. His timing was perfect.

Rukor snatched the scroll from my hand and without a word, spurred his horse and sped out of the courtyard with his knight and messenger following close on his heels.

Now we wait.

·CHAPTER 25·

"I think that pumping the Greek fire was the right thing to do," panted Spirus.

Father and I had discussed that decision at length. It was important for us not to appear to be threatening Rukor, but to warn him what the consequences of "no agreement" would be. To threaten him would work him into a blind fury and would compel him to attack without fear of consequence. Our Greek fire was a warning, a preview of an outcome we did not prefer. It was still left to be seen how it would be received.

To get some indication of Rukor's reaction to our plan, Father and I climbed our way to the tower to join Havark and Yoshi. They were on the lookout for the slightest indication that Rukor's men were ready to advance. Any such move would be greeted with a storm of fiery arrows from Havark's archers. I feared that Havark's fingers would be itching to release his signal. I started taking the steps three at a time.

"Meet me at the top," I said to Father.

I looked back to see him standing still, fighting to catch his breath.

"You… You go ahead. I am going to make my way back down," he said.

"That is probably best," I replied. "You need to be there if he returns."

After not having been up these steps for years, I found myself spiralling my way upwards for the second time in a week. It seemed easier this time. Perhaps my fear had released some inner strength.

"Anthos, is that you?" a voice called down to me.

"Yoshi, I am almost there," I answered.

With just a few more steps I could see Yoshi's silhouette in the entrance to the tower.

"Come on!" he shouted.

"Where's Havark?" I asked as I arrived at the door.

"Come," said Yoshi, "I need your help."

Yoshi grabbed me by the arm and pulled me to the tower's edge where Havark was leaning over the side to get a better view of the fields.

"I think he is going to attack," shouted Havark. "His men are holding formation. If we wait, it will be too late."

"No Havark!" said Yoshi. "Give him some time. He must have realised by now that we can torch the fields. If he were about to attack, he would not keep his men there. He would have moved them by now."

"I will not take that chance," yelled Havark. He pulled an arrow from his back and placed its wrapped tip into the flame of a ready torch.

Havark placed the lit arrow in his crossbow and started pulling the lever to lock it in place. I ran to him and kicked him behind the knee closest to me while Yoshi wrestled the crossbow from his hands. He fell to his knees and I pulled him to the ground and sat on his chest. The lit arrow from Havark's bow shot feebly into the ground, having not been properly locked into place before our intervention.

"Yoshi!" I shouted. "The arrow!"

Yoshi grabbed the flaming arrow and mounted it carefully into the bow. He moved to the edge of the tower and kept a lookout for any sign of aggression from Rukor's soldiers. He would not have hesitated to signal Havark's men if Rukor made the first move.

"Stop it, Havark!" I shouted. "You are taking this personally. Control yourself."

Havark glared at me with the rage of a wild animal. He offered no resistance although I knew that it would be a simple matter for him to throw me off.

"You have every right to be angry," I said. "But if you signal before it is time, nobody wins. We have a plan. Do not let your emotions get the better of you."

I felt the tension from his body ease away as he lay there without saying a word.

"Trust me, my brother," I said. "Rukor will ride back in. You may have your opportunity to torch his sorry soul, but not yet. Your men are counting on you to guide them."

"I am sorry, Anthos," he said. "But I just could not stand to see him talk to Father like that. I could not hear his words but his every action showed contempt."

"So what?" I said. "Let him puff up his chest. Father is not bothered. Do not bring your hatred from the past into today's dealings. Focus on the problem, not the person."

"Gentlemen," Yoshi intervened, "we will have an opportunity to do just that."

I jumped up and extended my hand to pull Havark to his feet.

"What is going on?" asked Havark, as we both rushed to the edge.

"Look," said Yoshi, "Rukor and his general are on their way back in."

·Chapter 26·

"It is everywhere," said Oleg.

"The fields are covered in it. The men as well."

One of Rukor's generals was reporting on what he had seen as he rode through the mist of a mysterious liquid that was being sprayed from wooden tubes protruding from the ground. As first, the men thought that it was just water, but the liquid clung to their skin and had a bitter taste as it ran into their mouths. By the time they started slashing away at the tubes with their swords it was too late. Everything in the field was coated and the warriors' skin glistened in the sun.

Rukor wiped his forefinger down the arm of his general and tasted the residue along its length.

"Spirus plans to burn the fields," he said.

"What?" said Oleg. "How do you know?"

"I am not aware of this liquid's nature, but I am convinced that it provides fuel for a flame," said Rukor.

"So they *did* know we were coming. But how?" asked Oleg.

Rukor looked down at the scroll in his hand.

"Impossible," he said. "We must have a spy."

"My Lord should read the scroll," said Oleg. "Maybe they are telling the truth."

"Silence!" shouted Rukor. "I need to think. Why have they not lit the fields? What are they waiting for?"

Oleg thought that the answer might be found in the scroll but he knew that a second interruption might be his last.

Rukor slowly unrolled the scroll and read it silently.

"Deep inside my mind I see,

A vision that is yet to be.

A fearless warrior takes control,

In with the new, out with the old.

This ruler rides without his shield,

His very name makes mortals yield.

His kingdom sits on mountain high,

While other lands attract his eye.

Precious metal comes from the ground,

But food to eat cannot be found.

While hunger makes his people drop,

Those other lands are filled with crops.

If he should move to stake his claim,

Those lands go up in burning flames.

But if he halts his heavy hand,

A special gift comes to his land.

From stony ground new life will sprout,

With blessings from the river trout.

And shining blades will find their worth,

In patterns that will turn the earth.

The mountain people start to cheer,

Their ruler saves them from despair.

But all these words will come to naught,

If men insist that war is fought.

So men of power, listen well,

You hold the door to your own Hell."

"How can this be?" Rukor asked himself. "They *did* know we were coming, and they have prepared for us. But this scroll predicts that I can be a hero to my people. Why would they want that? Why have they not set the fields on fire?"

Rukor handed the scroll over to Oleg without comment. His eyes lit up as he read it.

"Can this be real? How can this be real? This foretells crops growing on Apa's stony soil. That cannot be possible," said Oleg in disbelief.

"They have not told us everything," said Rukor. "But they are watching us. Instruct the men to hold formation. If we scatter, they will ignite the fields."

"Yes, my Lord." said Oleg.

As he was about to ride off to carry out his Lord's command, Rukor stopped him.

"Wait!" he shouted.

"My Lord?" said Oleg.

"The scroll," Rukor said, holding out his hand.

"I'm sorry, my Lord" Oleg handed Rukor the scroll before riding off.

"Come back here to meet me when you are through," Rukor yelled.

Rukor realised that he was trapped. Spirus would never have farmers in the fields knowing that they might burn with his enemy. Those men were soldiers in disguise and were likely to be ready to unleash their flames upon his warriors at the slightest indication of attack. Rukor would rather face certain defeat than be dishonoured in front of his men. Yet, the scroll spoke about Rukor being cheered by his people if war was avoided. He wondered how it would be possible for him to gain power without war. He opened the scroll and read it again.

"The mountain people start to cheer,

Their ruler saves them from despair."

"Let us see, King Spirus," he said. "Let us see what you have in mind."

·CHAPTER 27·

"What have you sprayed on my men?" asked Rukor.

"Your men have been sprayed only as a consequence of their position. That spray is intended for the crops," said Spirus.

"Keep that story for those who might believe it," said Rukor. "Where did you get this?"

Rukor thrust the scroll in Spirus' face.

"The origin of that scroll is of no importance," said Spirus. "The important thing for us both to consider is its contents."

"Father," I said, "I am here."

I had just arrived from the tower. After spending a moment at the bottom of the stairs to compose myself, I walked past our guards to find Rukor and his general, both on horseback, with Rukor pointing the scroll down at Father's face.

"This is your other son?" asked Rukor, looking at Spirus. "I wondered earlier who he was. What is his name? Is it Alexander or something like that?"

"You may address your questions to me," I said, "and my name is Anthos."

Rukor laughed.

"He has a fiery tongue, Spirus," he said. "Tongues like that usually get their owners' throats slit."

He made a motion across his own neck as if he were drawing a blade.

"Rukor," said Spirus, "now that we are past introductions, can I invite you to dismount and join me for a walk so we may speak?

"I do not trust you, Spirus," said Rukor. "You have proven yourself to be a devious man."

"I am just a man seeking solutions," said Spirus. "Please, walk with me. Bring your general. Anthos will accompany us as well."

Rukor and his general descended from their horses. His general began to unsheathe his sword, but Rukor signalled him to return it.

"This way," said Spirus, and pointed down a path towards the river.

Our guards moved hesitantly out of the way to let the four of us pass, and watched us walk out of their circle of protection. I retained some comfort knowing that Havark's keen eyes would be tracking our every move from the tower and he would respond immediately to the slightest threat.

"We have had the benefit of the knowledge in the scroll for some time," said Spirus. "Now that you have seen it, what are your thoughts?"

"It refers to me," said Rukor, "and my ability to retain power."

His main interest is retaining power!

When I composed the prophecy in the scroll, I embedded three subjects that would help me understand what Rukor held important. I included a verse that predicted food for his people, another that spoke about new worth for his shining blades and another about recognition by his people. It was the recognition that appealed to him the most. We would have to frame our discussions around his retention of power. I glanced over at Father and his subtle nod showed me that he understood.

"I understand the responsibility that comes with leading a kingdom of people who rely on you," said Spirus. "It is not an easy thing for those who have not experienced it to comprehend."

"What are you getting at?" snapped Rukor. He was getting impatient.

"Rukor, you and I have the same responsibility as rulers, except you have used your weapons to provide food for your people, while I have had the benefit of being able to grow my crops myself," said Spirus.

"You have only had that benefit because you have fertile land, something that I do not possess," said Rukor.

"Ahhh! But what if I told you that there was a way to grow crops on your stony soil? Would that interest you?" said Spirus.

"How can that be possible?" asked Rukor's general. These were the first words from his mouth.

"What is your name, sir?" I asked.

"My name is Oleg," he replied.

"Father, may I demonstrate?" I asked.

"Please do," he replied.

"Take a look over there," I said.

I pointed at a small pond that was visible in the distance. It was being artificially fed with water channelled from the river.

"That pond was created for us to try to breed trout," I said. "I have had problems with it. When the numbers of trout become too large, the pond becomes filled with their bloated corpses. I have been trying to figure out for a long time why this was happening."

"Have you come up with any ideas?" asked Oleg.

"I have," I said. "There are two reasons. First, as the number of fish in the pond increases, the amount of air in the water has to increase in order for them to survive. This water is being circulated too slowly and the fish are struggling to breathe in this artificial environment. Additionally, with larger amounts of fish, there is a larger amount of fish droppings that pollute and poison the water."

"So this is useless then," said Rukor.

"Not at all," I said. "By the time the Turok river passes through Cyden, its banks are wide and its waters meander slowly by. But up in Apa, the waters race through the mountains and are filled with oxygen. If these fast-moving waters are diverted into a fishpond and then fed back into the river, a rapid circulation will result. This will allow for the pond water to continuously be replenished at a rate that will ensure there is always oxygen-rich, fresh water in the pond. Under these conditions, a very large number of fish can be reared in a very small space."

"But what about the poisons from the waste?" asked Oleg. "That will be even worse with more fish in the pond."

"That is the best part," I said. "Come with me."

I stepped off the path and walked around the pond to a small area on its far side. There was an empty field filled with gravel.

"What is this?" asked Rukor. "There is nothing here."

"Take a closer look," I said.

Oleg stepped to the edge of the gravel and dropped on his hands and knees to inspect the field more closely.

"It's filled with seeds," he said, "and they are all sprouting."

He picked up a bean that had already taken root and was displaying a little green leaf like a victory flag.

"But how can these seeds take root? There is no soil," said Oleg.

Rukor stepped into the field and walked about four paces inside. He stooped to pick up one of the sprouting seeds and held it up to his face for a closer inspection.

"How did you do this?" he demanded.

"Can I see the scroll?" I asked.

Rukor handed me the scroll he had tucked under his arm. I unrolled it and read aloud.

From stony ground new life will sprout,

With blessings from the river trout.

"The very droppings that are poisonous to the fish provide extraordinary nourishment to the plants," I said. "So much so that soil is not necessary. These seeds were planted only two days ago. They have sprouted faster than any I have ever seen and will actually grow bigger and more quickly than if they were planted in dirt."

Oleg looked across at Rukor to gauge his reaction. He tried to suppress his excitement until he had some indication that Rukor shared his emotions.

"So you think this can work in Apa?" Rukor asked calmly.

"I have already drawn construction plans. Not only will your rapid waters provide the oxygen for the trout, it will also supply the power for a pumping system that will extract the droppings from the bottom of the ponds and deposit them on gravel beds for your crops."

"Lord Rukor, this is fantastic," said Oleg.

Rukor cast a silencing glare at his General. I could tell that he would rather conceal his opinions until he learnt more.

"How will we feed these fish?" asked Rukor. "These trout will need to be fed."

"You are correct, Lord Rukor," I said. "Let me show you something."

I walked over to a tree at the edge of the field and pulled down a device that was hanging from a branch.

"This simple apparatus will provide food for your fish while you sleep," I said.

I could see from Rukor's blank expression that he was not convinced.

"A small oil-lamp fits into this slot here," I continued, holding up my invention for Rukor to see.

"These are lit at night and suspended over your ponds. The light will attract insects and bugs to the device. As the insects circle the light, they strike these black panels and fall into the water. When several of these are strung over the ponds, they not only provide natural food for your fish, but control the amount of insects around your crops as well. It is one big cycle. Your plants will attract more insects, which will provide food for your fish, which will provide fertiliser for your plants."

Oleg could retain his excitement no longer.

"Lord Rukor, this is exactly what we need!"

"Let your Lord be the judge of that," Rukor snapped. "Why are you showing us this? What do you want in return?"

I looked down at the scroll and read again.

And shining blades will find their worth,

In patterns that will turn the earth.

"What does that mean?" asked Oleg.

"It is about your knowledge of metals," said Spirus.

Father had remained silent while I explained the fish fertiliser concept to Rukor and Oleg. He felt it was best to leave the explanation of technical plans to me. The time had come, however, when we were about to trade concessions and this required his authority.

"Please, let us continue this conversation back on the path," said Spirus. He could see that Rukor was still a little distracted by the pond.

"For centuries, farmers have known that crops grow more easily in soil that is ploughed." Spirus talked as he walked.

"A plough simply breaks up and turns over the soil. This process allows the sower to easily work the seed into the soil, and gives the planted seed more access to the water and air essential for its survival and growth."

We approached our stables as Father was speaking and I walked ahead to open the doors.

"Let me show you something Rukor," said Spirus.

Rukor stood motionless outside the door as Father stepped inside. Father and I knew that he would be more likely to make a final agreement in the privacy of a conference between two kings. We did not consider his distrust of being led into a closed space like the stable. Rukor had understood that his men were at our mercy in the fields. He would not want to put himself at the risk of an ambush in a dark enclosure.

Think quickly Anthos! He does not look like he will go inside!

This moment seemed like an eternity, but eventually, Rukor stepped towards the stable door.

"Oleg," he said. "Wait outside with the prince until I return."

Rukor knew that Spirus could easily have incinerated him in the fields with his men. We would have nothing to gain from killing him and leaving his men leaderless to panic in the fields. I guessed he understood that we were trying to reason with him. War was our last option, not our first.

Inside the stable, Spirus pointed to a wooden device leaning against the inner wall.

"That is a Roman plough," he said. "It is made of wood and is drawn by horses with a farmer's guidance."

"I am familiar with the concept," said Rukor.

"Excellent, then this will be simple," said Spirus.

"This plough only digs one furrow at a time and requires a significant amount of effort from the farmer. Anthos has been working on a design for a new plough, one made of metal. This new design can turn over the soil more efficiently, but more importantly, dig three furrows at the same time. His prototypes, however, have all failed. We have limited knowledge about the nature of metals so the blades of his new plough have either been too soft, and bent terribly out of shape with use, or been too brittle, and broke into pieces after only a few minutes."

"Ahhhh! You are learning that Lady Iron is a difficult damsel to charm," said Rukor with a knowing grin.

"More difficult than Anthos cares to admit," responded Spirus.

"Rukor, what we need from you is your expertise to produce this new plough. Anthos has designed it in three separate parts so broken blades can be changed without having to replace the entire plough. We know what is happening at Hagg with your weapons trade. This innovative device will give you a new area of proficiency that engages your blacksmiths in creating a tool that will always find buyers at Hagg. You will no longer have to depend solely on your weapons for your income."

"Let me understand this," said Rukor, "You are prepared to give me the plans for the fish pond in exchange for the production of your iron plough?"

"That is part of the deal," said Spirus. "You will benefit greatly from producing your own food, and although we will benefit from having new iron ploughs in our fields, you will be earning countless goldtriens from its trade. There is another concession to be made."

"Tell me what you want, Spirus," said Rukor.

"I want Jude to come over here to Cyden. I want him to serve as our resident blacksmith," said Spirus, "and I want his daughter Lia to accompany him."

"What?" Rukor roared. "You want my finest blacksmith! You must be out of your mind."

"Rukor, you have no buyers for your weapons. Jude will be designing new agricultural tools for your people to produce. He cannot develop those tools unless he has direct experience with their use in the fields. We will not be crafting the tools, you will. Jude will create their design and your blacksmiths will forge them in the mountains. He will serve your purpose more efficiently from afar."

Rukor kicked at a bale of hay and stomped towards Spirus.

"All right Spirus," he growled, "You will get your blacksmith, but his daughter stays in Apa."

"That is not acceptable!!!" Spirus raised his voice in a tone that I easily recognised from outside the stable. I had heard that voice many times as a boy.

"What use to me is a father grieving his separation from his only family," said Spirus. "Look, Rukor, you have an opportunity to be a hero to your people. We recognise that it will take some time for your first crops to bear produce, so we have prepared eighty cartloads of provisions in exchange for all of the weapons that your men are carrying now. You will march your soldiers back into Apa carrying food for their immediate needs, and a powerful strategy to enrich their lives. You will be greeted by cheers and adulations. This decision will seal your legacy as Apa's saviour and patron and will be recounted for generations."

The most important words of the scroll were clear in Rukor's mind.

The mountain people start to cheer,

Their ruler saves them from despair.

"Spirus…" said Rukor.

"Tell me, Rukor," said Spirus.

"You have my agreement," said Rukor after a lengthy pause.

Rukor extended his hand towards Spirus to seal his decision. Father accepted and returned the gesture. He knew that beneath Rukor's ego and aggression was the honour of a knight.

Rukor stepped out of the stable with Father at his side and shouted to Oleg.

"Oleg! Instruct the men to down their weapons. Prepare them for our withdrawal."

· EPILOGUE ·

"So this is where Havark kept watch over Rukor's men?" asked Lia.

"This is where he was seconds away from signalling our archers to put your crossbows to good use," I replied.

"Oh, Anthos," said Lia. "I am so sorry for running away in the middle of our meeting in Hagg. I felt terrible afterwards. I was just following Wheel's instructions."

"And Wheel was following instructions from my father," I said. "At the time, I had no idea who you were and how much of a risk you were taking to be there."

Lia and I were standing in the tower overlooking Cyden. I had just finished telling her the story of Rukor's agreement to withdraw his warriors from Cyden. Father knew the importance of getting Jude and Lia out of Apa, and had always intended to make it an integral part of his negotiations. He could not chance Rukor finding out about their involvement in getting us the very crossbows that might have been used to defeat him. He would not have spared their lives.

After Rukor's withdrawal we had more weapons than we knew what to do with. Havark and his men sifted through the stockpile to select the finest pieces and Father decided to destroy the rest. Four dozen of our men accompanied our food carts back to Apa to assist Rukor in the construction of the ponds. Lia had just given me an account of the hero's welcome that Rukor was given by his people when he rode in victoriously to relieve them from hunger. The families of his soldiers ran into the streets to account for their loved ones and were stunned to discover that not a single life was lost. Rukor was cheered for his brilliance.

Back in Cyden, my brilliance was being rewarded with the task of cleaning out the Greek fire from our entire irrigation system, as well as overseeing the reconstruction of the pipes that were damaged by Rukor's men. Some of our crops were also made inedible from being sprayed with the Greek fire so I had several weeks of hard labour in my future. I had to admit that having this moment with Lia made the burden seem a bit lighter.

"Do you think this will be the last we hear of Rukor?" Lia asked.

"I am not sure that anyone can predict what someone like Rukor will do," I said. "For now, he is rejuvenated and enjoying the adoration of his people. Who knows? Maybe that will satisfy his ego for a while. Maybe not. I believe that we have to continue to develop our relationship with Apa and find new ways to trade. We also need to build our army so we are not caught sleeping like we were this time. Havark will see to that. Rukor may not decide to attack us again, but there are other threats out there. We cannot be as complacent as we have been in the past."

"I still worry about him finding out about the crossbows," said Lia. "I have nightmares about opening my eyes in the middle of the night to find him standing over my bed."

I felt the back of my neck, fumbling nervously for the clasp of my necklace. I took it off and held it out towards her.

"A friend gave this to me and said it was for my protection," I said. "It provided comfort for me as I looked out into the fields and saw Rukor's men preparing to invade. I am sure that you are no longer in danger from Rukor. The only ones who know about our deal are on our side. I trust Wheel and Deal completely, and the innkeeper had no idea why you were there. I believe that he thought we were lovers."

Lia giggled.

"Why are you laughing? Is that so ridiculous?" I asked.

"If only he knew the truth," she said.

"Anyway," I continued, "the woman who gave this necklace to me said that I would know when the time was right to hand it over to someone else who might benefit from it. I have learnt not to question her wisdom. I would like you to have it."

"Anthos, that was a gift to you. I can not accept it," she said.

"It is not mine," I said. "I was just holding it for you."

I stepped behind her and placed it around her neck.

"This is just a small symbol of the beginning of a new day for you," I said.

"A new day for all of us."

II.

NEGOTIATION NOTES

NEGOTIATION:

a *voluntary* process
between two or more parties
who *exchange information* about their
needs and objectives in order
to reach *agreement* on one
or more issues

I.

What kind of Negotiator are you?

Why did King Spirus choose Anthos to go to Hagg, rather than Havark?

When faced with the reality of Rukor's attack, Spirus had to make a decision on which of his sons would be better suited to craft a solution for their situation. Havark was his physically stronger son and was naturally gifted in combat skills and warfare strategy. On the other hand, Anthos was a deep thinker and enjoyed solving problems. If he had to describe their personalities, Spirus might have called Havark highly competitive, and Anthos, a natural collaborator.

Just like Anthos and Havark, we all have a dominant, natural negotiating style. These natural styles affect how we instinctively approach a conflict or bargaining situation. However, no one is completely defined by any one particular approach. Several studies have described five basic categories of negotiating styles. People have a natural tendency to:

- **Avoid conflict.** Some people do not like confrontation and prefer to avoid negotiation situations. They tend not to complain if the food in a restaurant is bad, or will not ask for a discount when making a purchase. They may also avoid discussing a problem with a co-worker or spouse, and may find themselves being taken advantage of, or missing an opportunity to improve their situation.

- **Give in to the other party.** These individuals tend to yield to the wishes of others and will agree with them in order to avoid conflict. In some cases, they may not be in agreement with the position being put forward, but will still consent in order to keep the peace. They may feel that their relationship with the other party will be jeopardised if they do not see eye to eye, or may feel that the other side is too powerful to negotiate with.

- **Meet others halfway.** While this seems like an appropriate approach to solving differences, people who have this tendency will often settle on a less than optimum agreement. In most cases, creative thinking can find ways for both parties to get more value out of the deal than from just splitting the difference. There is a well-known story of two children fighting for an orange. Their mother decides to resolve the issue by cutting the orange in two and giving each child half. The mother later discovers that one child wanted the orange for its juice, while the other wanted its rind to bake a cake. In this instance, a compromise resulted in a loss of value for both sides.

- **Want to win.** We all know people who will argue every point and are driven to win at all costs. They try to gain all they can at the other party's expense. These are typically the individuals who use intimidation, pressure and other tactics to influence a decision in their favour. While these actions may give them an immediate victory, they often damage relationships and make other parties withdraw. When two highly competitive parties meet, egos rule and there is often no agreement.

- **Solve the problem.** These "problem-solvers" will try their best to find a win-win solution for every negotiation scenario. They tend to share information openly, and will pose fact-finding questions to the other side. Underlying interests are important to these individuals in order for them to see the big picture and they see the problem as the adversary, rather than the other party.

You should reflect on these differing styles and determine which one describes you best. One way of getting a clear idea of your personal conflict management style is with the Thomas-Kilmann Conflict Mode Instrument. This tool asks thirty questions and then assigns a score on a scale of 0-12 for five different styles: Avoiding, Accommodating, Compromising, Competing and Collaborating. This test is available from Consulting Psychologists Press, Inc. at www.cpp-db.com. Of course, everyone will have aspects of *all* these tendencies as part of their personality, but you will find that one or two styles dominate your typical behaviour in conflict situations. The challenge is to recognise your natural negotiating style, and know when the situation calls for a shift to a more problem-solving or collaborative technique. Some scenarios may be trivial and an "avoidance" approach may be the most appropriate. Other cases may call for you to become more competitive. However, you should always determine whether there is any benefit to be gained from exploring the opportunity to create mutual gains for yourself and the other party.

As a natural collaborator, Anthos prepared for his negotiation with Rukor by creating strategies that explored their mutual interests and brought gains to both sides. Does that mean that if Havark was chosen he would not have done the same? As a natural competitor, it might have been more difficult for him. However, he would have had to adjust his natural behaviour to a style that was more appropriate to the situation.

We all have the capacity to become more collaborative. The challenge is to recognise the need for a behavioural shift if collaboration is not our natural style, and if necessary, to apply a problem-solving approach to the issues being negotiated.

2.

Power, Information and Time

How did King Spirus plan to negotiate with a more physically powerful aggressor?

One definition of power is simply your ability to get what you want.

The first form of power is that of **threat**. This source of power can come from one's position of authority, ability to punish or physical strength. This was clearly the power that Rukor was demonstrating in his threatened attack on Cyden with his dominant army. Individuals can also have dominance over others through an emotional threat using anger, crying or silence to get their way.

A second source is the power of **trade**. This comes from the possession of resources that are perceived as valuable by the other party. These assets give you the power to exchange them for resources that *you* consider valuable from other parties. Resources can be physical items, but are also intangibles like skills, intellect, expertise or knowledge. Spirus knew that this was the type of power that he would have to use in order to negotiate effectively with Rukor. Anthos used his intellect and expertise in farming to develop creative solutions for Rukor's problems, and used this power to trade for peace and for Jude's skills as a blacksmith.

Thirdly, there is the power of **relationship**. This power can influence others through bonds or emotional ties that connect them to someone. People often have influence over others through ethnic, cultural, social, class or family bonds. They can also influence others by their charisma or charm. Anthos was assisted by many individuals in Hagg because of the good relationships they had with Spirus and Cyden's traders. He was also somewhat charismatic and humble in his interactions, which built his relationship power.

While "power" can be used to describe one's ability to get their way, "leverage" can describe how this power shifts according to time or the specifics of the situation. Anthos received a lesson in leverage when Deal purchased the boots from Rafeek. Deal reduced Rafeek's power to trade by disguising the fact that Anthos *needed* the boots. She used Wheel's sandals as leverage in the deal to increase her negotiating power.

A typical example of changing leverage can be found in a job offer. When the applicant is being interviewed, the company has more leverage, as interviewees do not know how they measure up against the other applicants. If an offer is made to the applicant, that leverage shifts in the period *before* they accept or reject the job offer. This is the period of greatest negotiating power for the applicant, which quickly fades the moment the job is accepted. The applicant's best opportunity to negotiate their package is during that period of increased power.

In response to Rukor's strength, King Spirus planned for his negotiation by building both his power of *threat* and his power of *trade*. He did not consider the option suggested by Havark, to create additional power by seeking allies, but instead, built his physical capacity to overcome Rukor's army through the use of Greek fire. In this way, he overcame Rukor's power of threat, even though he decided to use this force only as an alternative. The use of allies, however, is a common strategy to generate the power of threat. Even children understand this, and can sometimes enlist one parent to support their cause against the other.

Spirus preferred to achieve his desired outcome through the power of trade. Anthos used his expertise to create valuable options that Rukor could not ignore. Similarly, jobseekers build their technical skills and experience to increase their power in the eyes of employers.

Finally, Anthos recognised the need to improve the power of *relationship* with Rukor in order to ensure that the peace was lasting. A party's power structure always consists of varying degrees of these three components, and the negotiator's challenge is to improve their overall position by enhancing their strengths while neutralising those of the other side.

Did Cyden build their Power using Information?

King Spirus and his forefathers placed a great value on **information** as they recognised its power in developing solutions for their problems. Several issues must be considered when building negotiating power through information:

- Collect as much information as possible about the other party and their interests *before* any interaction,

- Be very careful about how you reveal information about yourself and your interests,

- Use any information you have to develop creative solutions,

- Carefully listen and observe to identify all the information the other party reveals to you during the negotiation.

The initial warning from Martol was an essential piece of information that allowed Spirus to start developing a plan. Yoshi then used historical information from their archives to craft a feasible alternative if the negotiations failed. Anthos needed to understand as much as he could about Rukor's interests. He gathered some information from Dowan at Hagg, but also carefully listened to Rukor's comments in response to his "prophecy".

The important lesson here is that it is essential, both before and during any negotiation, to collect as much relevant information as possible. This will ensure that you consider all your options for creating the most favourable outcome. For example, there has been a shift in the balance of power between parties selling and buying a car in the United States. Sellers try to refer to the MSRP (Manufacturer's Suggested Retail Price) on the sticker as their starting price, however, buyers can now readily access information on the seller's invoice cost, and reframe their negotiation in terms of the amount they are prepared to pay above that cost. The Internet has revolutionised access to information and can provide comprehensive research on the other parties and the issues being negotiated. Here are a few tips on using search engines, particularly Google™, to find information on the Internet.

- Use quotation marks to search for specific phrases.

- Look out for spelling mistakes. Consider the difference between British and American English spelling (organisation vs. organization).

- Use the singular form of your search word.

- Don't use words like "how", "the" and "I". They will be ignored.

- Word order matters so place more important search terms ahead of others.

- Search for specific file types like Microsoft Word™, Powerpoint™, or Adobe Acrobat™ PDF by adding – filetype: plus the file extension. For example to find a Word™ document, use filetype:doc.

- Use Boolean operators to construct search statements (AND, OR, NOT, etc...)

- Consider using the research specialists at Google Answers™. Prices range between $2.00 and $200.00 depending on the level of detail you require. Previously researched topics are archived and accessible for free.

- Try using a simplified third-party interface for more advanced searches like Soople.com.

Why was Rukor's demand for immediate surrender ignored by King Spirus?

Negotiators must use **time** to their advantage. The party that uses time to gather information, probes the other side for their interests and appears less eager for a settlement, will usually have a better outcome.

Spirus understood that negotiations begin long before the parties get together and used the time he had wisely, to prepare for Rukor's arrival. When someone is pressing you for a decision, it is always wise to slow them down. Take time to slow down your thoughts, to comprehend the issues carefully and to elucidate your responses clearly.

You should also be aware of differences in the value of time in inter-cultural negotiations. Americans tend to take a "time is money" approach to deal-making and are often frustrated by the slow pace of transactions when conducting business in other cultures. It would not be unusual for a Mexican businessman to want to do some sight-seeing, dining and talking a bit about family before even looking at a contract, while an American might prefer to sign the contract first, and then get on with any socialising. In many cultures, businessmen prefer to do business with "friends" and will want to spend some time getting to know their counterparts before making any agreements.

In addition, be wary of deadlines. They are often created to force a decision from you. Direct marketers know this principle well and their offer will often expire by a specified deadline. They may also create an illusion of a limited supply of product to imply the need for urgency. Spirus ignored Rukor's immediate deadline for a decision because he knew that it was not real. It was unilaterally set by Rukor to force Spirus into a corner. Spirus slowed the conversation down to allow for solutions to be found for the real problems Rukor was facing, which were the genuine issues behind his demands.

3.

Negotiation Tactics

What did Anthos learn about negotiation tactics in Hagg?

Anthos encountered several well-known negotiation tactics during his visit to Hagg. You are likely to experience them as well in your negotiations. The first step in handling these tactics is recognising them. Let us look at some of the more commonly encountered ones.

Anchoring effect

In every negotiation, one party has to make the first offer, and this will almost always have an impact on the final outcome of the agreement. In addition, negotiators who set high targets usually achieve better outcomes than those who do not. The effect of an anchor, or the first offer introduced into a negotiation, is that it creates a reference point around which concessions will be made. By making the first offer, you are likely to anchor the negotiation in your favour.

Of course, there is always the concern that any first offer will be too extreme and may result in the other side walking away from the negotiation. This underscores the importance of preparation and ensuring that you have gathered enough information to make your offer aggressive but not absurd. It would also be useful to learn about the other party's alternatives to your offer.

In one salary negotiation I was involved in, I referred to objective standards in a salary survey to set my outlook. I made a mistake by allowing my prospective employer to make the first offer which was significantly lower than my expectation. I found myself negotiating around their initial offer, which was anchored much lower than my target, and was not able to achieve a satisfactory outcome until I reframed the negotiation around other issues, and was able to break away from their initial proposal. In the end, I met my target, but took a great risk by allowing my employer to anchor the discussion around a low figure. You should always focus on your target outcome and give yourself enough room to give up some concessions to the other side. Not only will this approach result in a better outcome for you, but it will leave the other side satisfied that they have made some gains in the process.

Deal was very careful to anchor the price of Anthos' boots at twenty coppers. If she had allowed Rafeek to open at seventy, they would have likely settled at a much higher price. She effectively anchored the price close to her target of thirty coppers, knowing that it was a fair price for the boots.

Splitting the Difference

The seller offers a price of $100,000 to the buyer's opening of $60,000. The seller suggests, "Why don't we split the difference and settle at $80,000? That seems fair." But it might not be. The seller may have anchored his price unrealistically at $100,000, and $80,000 might still be too much to pay.

What if the seller's initial offer had been $80,000? Then splitting the difference would put the price at $70,000. Splitting the difference is only as fair as the figures that are being split. It is often a trap used when one party knows that their figure is unreasonable, and splitting the difference would still give them an advantage while appearing to be fair. If the seller insists on splitting the difference, there is nothing to stop the buyer from saying, "I would like to consider your new proposal of $80,000. Why don't we see if we can split the difference between $80,000 and $60,000, and settle this thing at $70,000?" Any offer to split the difference is a demonstration of willingness to make concessions. You just need to ensure that the concessions are in your favour.

The key lesson here is to always base your negotiations on your goal, not on parameters set by the other party.

Flinching

Assume at all times that the other party is extracting information from your responses. This does not just mean what you say, but your posture, your tone of voice, your facial expressions; everything about your body language. If they put an offer in front of you and your reaction is indifferent, they will assume that their offer is acceptable and an anchor may be established. Always flinch at the other party's first offer. This communicates to them that you are looking for a concession from them, and very often one will follow. This is especially likely if their offer was pitched beyond their true expectation. Rafeek tried to flinch at Deal's initial offer of twenty coppers for the boots. Deal, however, saw through his theatrics and ignored his protests.

I remember looking at a movie awards show that featured a category called, "Best Dramatic Pause". Do not underestimate the power of silence. It can be just as powerful as a display of shock or surprise. The key lesson is to leave your ego at home. I have witnessed negotiators who do not flinch because they do not want to appear "cheap" when a seller presents a price. Be cheap! Some of the wealthiest people in the world are. Why shouldn't you?

Good Cop, Bad Cop

This tactic is named after an interrogation technique made popular by detective movies. The first cop is aggressive and physically intimidating to the suspect, and then is called out of the room. A second cop then offers the suspect some coffee, maybe a cigarette, and almost apologises for his colleague's behaviour. He is friendly and tells the suspect that he is on his side. "Just tell me who pulled the trigger and I'll see what I can do for you."

I've used this tactic myself. During a vacation in China, my wife and I had a routine with the vendors in the market: if she saw something interesting, she would show it to me and ask for my opinion. Whether I liked it or not, I would think for a bit, then express my disapproval. I had a little code that I would use to let her know that I actually *liked* the item, I would tell her, "I'm not sure about this." She would then put the item down and look at me. I would shake my head, and the price would immediately begin to fall. Calculators would come out with the vendors asking, "How much do you want to pay?"

As obvious as this tactic might seem, it can be very subtle at times. Sometimes the "bad cop" is not even part of the negotiation, but is an unavailable supervisor or colleague. Rafeek tried using his mysterious brother Salmaan as the "bad cop" to encourage Anthos and Deal to complete their transaction with him. Deal simply ignored his attempts and demonstrated her willingness to complete her business with Salmaan the next day.

The best defence for this tactic is first of all to recognise it, and to subtly let the other party know that you are aware of what they are doing. You should not let it have any influence on your decisions. Be careful not to embarrass them with your allegation, as they may stick to their guns to validate their behaviour.

Decoys

People sometimes use unimportant issues as distractions in their negotiations in order to divert attention away from the real issues. Negotiators will occasionally introduce phoney demands that they will subsequently withdraw in exchange for concessions from the other side.

The "red herring" that Deal mentioned to Anthos after purchasing his boots is an example of this. The ethics of this tactic are questionable, and Deal ensured that her initial interest in the tunics was not seen as an unethical move on her part by purchasing one of them for Anthos along with the boots.

The disadvantage of introducing decoys into a transaction is that it prevents a problem-solving approach to the negotiation. The other party cannot identify or create solutions if they are not aware of what your true interests are. Decoys are also very difficult to recognise and can lead to stalemates or deadlocks. If you suspect that someone is using a decoy, you should try to question its importance more deeply and attempt to reframe the discussion around the key issues of the negotiation.

Higher Authority

In some instances, it is useful *not* to have the final authority in a negotiation. Individuals who have this power can sometimes be pressured into making an immediate decision by a persuasive counterpart. Even people who *do* possess this authority can appoint it to a committee or panel in order to minimise the risk of falling victim to high-pressure tactics. Lia effectively used this approach on Anthos when he was pressuring her to reduce her price on the arrows. She referred to a higher authority on whose behalf she was conducting the negotiations. She wisely shifted the "power to decide" out of her control.

At one point in my career, I was the marketing manager for a financial institution. I was always flooded by donation and sponsorship requests from hundreds of organisations. While the company I represented had a genuine interest in finding appropriate charitable causes to support, many of the requests were totally disconnected from the objectives of the marketing department or beyond our budget allocation. The only way I could effectively deal with the weekly calls from individuals lobbying for their cause was to refer the matter to a "sponsorship committee." This was the higher authority appointed by me to decide on such matters. Often, someone would ask to speak to my managing director in order to escalate the request, but wisely, my boss would refer them back to the committee. This committee provided leverage to deal with unrealistic or high-pressure demands. At times when people forced me for an immediate decision I would respond, "If you need an immediate decision, then you're making it easy for me to say no. However, if you wait for the committee's evaluation of your request, you may find yourself with a positive response. No promises." Amazingly, the need for an immediate decision would disappear.

When faced with any negotiation, you should clearly establish the authority of the negotiating party *before* talks begin. It may turn out that the party you are in discussions with has no deciding power and your role is to get them to make a compelling recommendation to the true decision-maker. Never depend on someone else to close a deal on your behalf, unless you specifically enlist them for their negotiation or mediation skills. You should make your best effort to conduct negotiations with the highest deciding authority possible from the other party.

4.

Splitting the Pie

Why was Anthos unable to reach an agreement with Lia for the arrows?

Often, negotiations are centred on a single issue, like the price of an item, and any gain for one party represents a loss for the other. The parties can be thought of as splitting a "fixed pie." This type of negotiation is called distributive, win-lose, value-claiming or zero-sum. These negotiations are characterised by initial bids, walk-away bids and target bids. Each party's goal is to get agreement as close as possible to the other side's walk-away bid, thus getting the best deal for themselves. Strategies include disguising your walk-away point while trying to uncover that of the other party.

Consider two possibilities in a distributive negotiation: Is the pie really fixed or do opportunities exist for it to be expanded? What happens if there is no zone of possible agreement?

To answer the first question, let me share another personal experience from the Chinese marketplace. I was haggling with a vendor over the price of a leather cell-phone holder. This is a classic distributive negotiation where any reduction in the price would be a gain for me at his expense. After we reached a satisfactory figure, I purchased the item, continued shopping and returned to my hotel to meet the twelve other friends who were on tour with my wife and me. When I showed them my new leather holder, they all wanted to get one. One of my friends even expressed an interest in buying a large quantity for wholesale distribution when he returned home. It occurred to me that this simple fixed-pie negotiation could have been expanded to bring mutual gains to both me and the vendor. I could have offered to return with my twelve friends, and if they purchased over ten cases, I would get one free. This pie was not fixed at all! The question was: did I have the time, or was I prepared to make the effort to explore this further? Maybe I should have, but I did not think of it at the time. The point is that you should not make the assumption that any negotiation is "fixed-pie" since there may be opportunities for mutual gain. This is provided, of course, that the stakes are worth your effort and time. Experienced negotiators always ensure that they get their fair share of the "pie," but they look for ways to expand it first.

For the second consideration, let us re-examine Anthos' purchase of the crossbows and his failed negotiation for the arrows. Both these cases involved the *single issue* of price. Anthos was able to come to an agreement for the crossbows because he was prepared to pay higher than Lia's walk-away price.

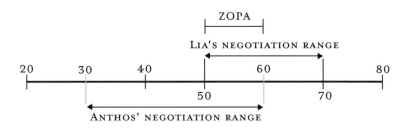

· FIGURE 1 ·

Figure 1 illustrates Anthos' opening bid of thirty coppers and his intention to walk-away at any price over sixty coppers. His initial bid was intended to anchor the negotiation at a low figure, and his high bid was determined by the number of coins he thought he would need to get the arrows afterwards. Lia opened at seventy, and we have made an assumption that her walk-away was fifty coppers. We can see that there is an overlap between the lowest figure Lia was prepared to accept and the highest that Anthos was prepared to pay. This overlap is referred to as the zone of possible agreement or ZOPA. Usually in a distributive negotiation, the wider the ZOPA, the greater the chance of reaching a negotiated agreement. This particular deal was settled at the upper limit of Anthos' negotiating range (his walk-away price) due to his inexperience, over-confidence and lack of information on the price he would be asked to pay for the arrows afterwards.

The transaction for the arrows, however, did not reach a conclusion as there was no ZOPA (refer to Figure 2).

NO ZOPA EXISTS

| 20 | 30 | 40 | 50 | 60 | 70 | 80 |

ANTHOS' MAXIMUM OFFER   LIA'S NEGOTIATION RANGE

· FIGURE 2 ·

The maximum Anthos could pay was twenty coppers, based on his unfortunate loss at the river, as well as the amount he had spent on the previous transaction. Lia was not prepared to accept less than sixty coppers, so no ZOPA existed. Is there anything Anthos could have done in order to reach an agreement in this case? Probably not, since Lia was purposely trying *not* to complete the sale. However, in typical selling negotiations, there are several non-price issues that can be introduced when a lack of agreement on price threatens to prevent the sale. These might include, for example:

· The terms of payment could be adjusted to allow for credit facilities or early payment concessions,

· Increased purchase volumes might justify a lower price,

· Extended contract periods,

· Changes to the product or service specifications,

· Delivery time. A service, for example can be scheduled for a slow period,

· Shipping or financing costs may be adjusted.

In essence, the challenge is to introduce other value-added issues when there is no ZOPA around a single issue like price. By introducing more than one issue, you are creating a mutual gains scenario from a win-lose scenario.

Overall, in a distributive negotiation, it is advantageous to adopt a more competitive style. Your goals should be set high, leaving room for making concessions. In setting your goals, remember the acronym S.M.A.R.T. Your goals should be Specific, Measurable, Action-oriented, Realistic, and have a Timeframe. When you are perfectly clear on what you are trying to achieve you will have an increased likelihood of success, and will not easily be influenced by tactics introduced by the other side. You should also offer concessions thoughtfully. Here are some guidelines to making concessions.

- Make your opening offer realistically high (or low) based on information gathered *before* your negotiation.

- Do not give any concession away for free, even if it has little value. You may not be aware of its worth to the other party.

- Do not appear too keen to make concessions. For example, avoid saying, "Well... the price is $80,000 but let's talk and see what we can come up with." Be aware that conceding too quickly may make the other side apprehensive and that getting a deal too easily is sometimes unrewarding.

- Consider a "tapered" approach to concessions. Start small to test the level of reciprocity from the other party, increase the relative value of your concessions according to those offered from the other side, then reduce the increments gradually as you reach your limit. The *way* you concede can be more important than *what* you concede.

- Don't be too eager to accept the other party's first concession. You may be giving up the opportunity to get a better deal, or you may make the other side feel that they have given you too much.

- Make sure that the other party understands the value of your concessions.

- Be careful not to concede too much as a deadline approaches.

- Be prepared to withdraw a concession if you feel that it has not been appropriately reciprocated or if you have made a mistake. If you have to withdraw a concession, it should be done with mutual consent and with the understanding that the terms for the concession were not met.

5.

Expanding the Pie

How did Dowan's ruling in the case of the sheep prepare Anthos to create options for solving Cyden's crisis?

In every negotiation, your challenge is to expand the pie, then maximise your share. Expanding the pie, or integrative negotiation, is also called win-win, mutual gains or value creating. This is done by examining multiple issues, then identifying how the party values these issues. You will find that people have different perceptions on the value of the issues on the table, and these differences can create opportunities for creative solutions that produce winning results for both sides. If you can trade off on issues that have *little* value to you, but high value to the other side, and receive concessions from them that have *great* value to you but little to them, then you have expanded the pie in a manner that creates fantastic opportunities for mutual gain. Remember, however, you still have to be skilful in ensuring that you get your fair share of the expanded pie. Your aim is to settle on an agreement that is *great* for you, and *good* for them.

Negotiators often come to the table with firm *positions*, or their ideal, unilateral solution to a dispute. It is, however, their needs, desires, hopes and fears that serve as motives for their positions. These are defined as their *interests*. In the case of Dowan's ruling on how to divide the two sheep between Alfred and Uric, they both held very different interests for the use of the sheep. They each maintained their position of getting **both** sheep for themselves, but Dowan's focus on the underlying interests behind those positions revealed that they placed different values on the attributes of the sheep. Alfred placed great value on the milk, but little on the wool, while Uric sought the wool with little consideration for the milk. With a little creative thinking, Dowan was able to find a solution that allowed both men to achieve their goals with an agreement that was significantly better than just splitting the pie by giving each man a single sheep.

As a negotiation becomes more complex with varying interests and multiple issues, finding solutions becomes a bit more challenging, but there is also greater opportunity for mutual gain. The following steps are essential to an integrative approach to negotiation.

- You have to be clear on your interests and have as much information as possible on the interests of the other parties. Look beyond their stated positions to understand what their true issues are. Rukor's position was to attack Cyden, however, his interests were really maintaining his position of power in Apa, feeding his citizens, and trading iron and its by-products.

- Information has to be shared thoughtfully in order to create options for expanding the pie through brainstorming. Probe for more information from the other side and decide how much of your information you are prepared to reveal depending on their cooperation. You may have to disclose something first in order to build trust. Be aware that they may not be totally honest in what they reveal. Try to confirm their data by independent means if possible.

- Parties need to determine fair principles for dividing the pie. Objective standards are often useful at this stage. Additionally, some of the strategies of distributive negotiation can be beneficial in claiming your fair share.

- Be firm on the achievement of your goals but flexible on the way they are achieved. There are many means to an end.

Anthos learnt the value of looking beyond Rukor's position of attacking Cyden, and started considering the underlying interests behind his actions. He knew that Rukor would not easily volunteer any information so he created value adding options on his own. He also created a fictitious third-party by presenting a "prophecy" to Rukor that gave a sense of objectivity to his suggestions.

Getting the other side to share information is not always a simple task. It requires some skill in the disciplines of *questioning* and *listening*. These skills are not all that easy to perfect. They take practice. The type of conversation where someone freely exchanges information with you does not tend to occur naturally on its own. It needs to be created with the right questions. There is a poem written by Rudyard Kipling that goes:

"I kept six honest serving men.

They taught me all I knew.

Their names are What and Why and When

and How and Where and Who."

These are sometimes referred to as the "5 Ws and H", and are types of open-ended questions that encourage the other side to share information with you. You can then probe further with more specific questions, that require direct answers.

In the salary negotiations that I described earlier, when I was told what the offer was, rather than comment on it, I asked, "How was that salary determined?" My employer went on to give me a fair amount of information about the level of the position and the way the salary was matched to the job description. This information was critical for me to negotiate further as I realised that my objective was not to haggle over the figure, but to shift the job description to the level I expected. I reframed the negotiation around the position, rather than the salary, and was able to eventually settle on a mutually beneficial agreement.

Listening is another vital negotiating skill. Many of us like to speak. We have a hard time listening. We hear the beginning of a person's story, then quickly figure out what they are going to say next, or how the story is going to end, and either mentally drift out of the conversation or interrupt with a story of our own. We often do not pay attention to the non-verbal cues that we receive from the speaker. This is even worse when we are trying to do something else during the conversation. How many times have you heard, "Go ahead, I'm listening to you", while the person checks their e-mail or looks at a document while you are speaking.

Anthos paid very close attention to Rukor's feedback on the scroll. He was able to determine that retention of power was the most important issue to him. Anthos also paid close attention to Rukor's body language and was immediately able to detect his concern for safety when Spirus asked him to follow into the barn. Here are some points on how you can improve your listening skills.

- Prepare to listen. Remove any distractions, like your cell phone, the television or your computer. Effective listening is a decision!

- Do not make any assumptions. Try to eliminate any of the following perceptual distortions:

  o *Stereotyping*: ascribing attributes to someone based on their appearance, behaviour or the group they belong to;

  o *Filtering*: selectively discounting things you do not agree with or understand;

  o *Projecting*: assuming the speaker shares your characteristics or feelings.

- Acknowledge without agreeing. Be attentive and maintain eye contact.

- Try not to interrupt. Allow the speaker to complete their thoughts.

- Avoid sending negative non-verbal cues. Don't roll your eyes, frown or fold your arms.

- Do not let negative emotions affect you. It is often difficult to control your anger, however, resist the temptation to strike back. Slow the conversation down in your mind. If necessary, excuse yourself and return when you are calm.

· Restate to confirm. Ensure you understand the message by paraphrasing back to the speaker when they have finished.

Every negotiation is a combination of *distributive* and *integrative* elements, and at times your best efforts to find opportunities for mutual gain will be met with resistance. You may have to become more competitive and aim to maximise the value that you can claim. However, if the stakes are important enough, you should always explore the potential for a true win-win outcome by expanding the pie through an integrative approach.

6.

Do You have an Alternative?

How did Greek fire strengthen King Spirus' negotiating power?

Choice is good! Have you ever dealt with a monopolistic business, for example, a sole cable provider for your area? They brandish a certain power knowing that you have no alternative. Take it or leave it! Having no alternative always reduces your negotiating power.

Fisher and Ury, in their 1981 publication "Getting to Yes", introduced the term BATNA, or **B**est **A**lternative **T**o a **N**egotiated **A**greement. This simply requires you to ask yourself, "What is the best outcome for me if I do not negotiate?" Clearly, you should never accept a negotiated agreement that is not as good as a result you can achieve *without* negotiating.

Spirus built a powerful BATNA using Greek fire. If he chose not to negotiate with Rukor, he had the option of annihilating Apa's army under a fiery mist. He built his "power of threat" as an alternative to a negotiated agreement with Rukor. The clear objective of Spirus' negotiation was to create an outcome that was better than that of his use of Greek fire. His ultimate goal was to protect his people from attack, his secondary goal was to rebuild a working relationship with Apa. Greek fire would satisfy the first goal, however, would have a high cost in lives, crops, machinery and hatred. On the other hand, Greek fire provided the leverage that Spirus needed to bring Rukor to the negotiating table.

Powerful BATNAs need to be developed. If you are buying a house, for example, you need to explore all the properties that meet your criteria and select from the alternatives. Even when you have a preferred property, it strengthens your position when there is a second property that you also like. As a seller, your BATNA will come from multiple offers on the property from interested buyers. Remember to think outside the box. In the earlier example of the sole cable provider, a BATNA can be built from satellite TV; if you're looking for a place to live you can always rent instead of purchasing a house; jobseekers can consider starting their own business rather than accepting an unattractive job offer. No matter what the situation, always look for opportunities to improve your BATNA.

What about the other side? What will *they* do if no agreement is reached? The power of your BATNA is only relative to theirs. You should think carefully about the other side's alternatives if no agreement is reached. Gather as much information as you can *before* the negotiation begins, then probe the other side to come to a reasonable conclusion on their BATNA.

Should you expose your BATNA to the other side? Reveal it only when it is more powerful than the other party thinks it is. Spirus let Rukor know the consequences of non-agreement by spraying his men with Greek fire. It was important not to appear threatening in revealing this potential as there was always the risk of Rukor's ego driving a self-defeating desire to win at any cost.

It may be possible that no real BATNA exists. If there's that one job that you truly desire above all others, that one dream home or even that single soul-mate that in your mind has no substitute, you may not see the value of having an option that you have no desire for. I have found that even in those cases where your BATNA may not serve as a walk-away measure, you can still build negotiating leverage through the strength of a powerful alternative; otherwise you put yourself at the mercy of the other party. Your offer may even lose value in their eyes if they perceive that you have no other choices.

7.

Getting a Third-party involved

How did Dowan's role as an arbitrator influence Anthos' idea to create the "prophecy"?

Alfred and Uric were arrested for fighting in the marketplace over the only two ewes available for sale in Hagg. This fight probably started when they reached a point in their dispute where they felt that no further advancement was possible. This is referred to as an impasse. In some cases, the impasse can be over a single issue, so discussions can continue on other issues, with the intention of returning to the unresolved matter at a later time. However, an impasse can sometimes bring an entire negotiation to a halt. In these instances, involving an impartial third-party is one of the most effective ways to restart talks and find a potential solution for the deadlock.

Dowan's role in Hagg was that of an arbitrator. In arbitration, disputing parties present their case to a third-party who examines all of the facts and makes a decision that is binding. Mediation, on the other hand, is a more cooperative process where the mediator facilitates face-to-face meetings of the parties to assist *them* in reaching a mutually-acceptable agreement themselves. When disputing parties seek a third-party for either mediation or arbitration, they usually select an expert on the topic in dispute. Dowan established his expertise in trading disputes through his experience as a trader, as well as his documentation of precedents set in previous cases. In fact, the legal systems of many countries are based on the principle of *stare decisis*. That is, legal precedent establishes the law.

Parties often negotiate with different perspectives on disputed issues. They may be influenced by their personal experience, incomplete or inaccurate information, or by an emotional bias. Making reference to objective third-party information can help to set standards on which all sides can agree and can have the same impact as using a person to intervene. These can be based on statistically significant research findings, for example, using a market survey to determine a salary. More subjective data can also be useful, such as, determining a fair price for real estate by making reference to the classified advertisements.

Anthos knew that Rukor would not be easily persuaded to negotiate anything other than Cyden's surrender. Spirus on the other hand, had no intention of surrendering. To avoid an impasse, Rukor needed to be enticed into considering non-aggressive options. The "prophecy" was created to imply that the alternatives to war were expressed by an unbiased prophet who only foretold what he had seen. When Anthos was with Dowan in Hagg, he realised that even hostile parties appear willing to listen to reason when an objective third-party becomes involved. No such party existed who might influence Rukor, so Anthos created one by using the scroll. In the early stages of the negotiation, Rukor was more likely to have been persuaded by this than by Spirus' efforts. He also believed that Spirus had gained an advantage by using this information to prepare for his attack. This gave him further confidence in the scroll's validity and made him more disposed to consider the implications of its words.

We may question the ethics of Anthos' decision in respect to our real-life situations. In nature, deception is often used by animals to ward off attacks from predators. Many butterflies have eyespots that lure predators to attack non-vital parts of their bodies, like the edge of their wings. When attacked, they escape by flying away with only a slightly damaged wing. Similarly, Anthos felt justified in using deception to avoid Rukor's attack. The alternative would have been a deadly battle, creating dire consequences for both sides.

Ensure that any objective criteria presented to you are, in fact, accurate and can stand up to public scrutiny. The most important thing is that all sides agree on the validity of the standards. You need to consider whether the information is relevant to the current situation and is not dated or out of context. Make certain that you are not being unduly influenced by time constraints or the charisma of a negotiator on the other side.

8.

Negotiating with Difficult People

How did Spirus create an environment for effective communication with the non-cooperative Rukor?

Difficult negotiators are hard to avoid. In a perfect world, we would all deal with collaborative counterparts who willingly cooperate to find opportunities for mutual gain. However, many individuals equate strong negotiation skills with aggressive, domineering and sometimes threatening behaviour. They place a high value on getting what they want with little concern for relationships. There can be several sources of difficulty:

- **The personality or attitude of the negotiator**

  Someone may be abrasive or obnoxious, and be difficult even if their concerns are practical or valid.

- **An unreasonable position or demand from the other side**

  Regardless of the qualities of the individual, their position may be difficult or impossible.

- **The method of communication may cause difficulties**

  Using an intermediary, for example, may cause misunderstandings or incorrect assumptions.

- **The situation may be inflammatory**

  For instance, emotions may run high as in the case of two motorists arguing over a traffic accident.

These factors often contribute to difficult situations that lead to impasse or in the worst instance, attack. Parties may get locked into their positions or deviate from key issues. There can be non-cooperation and hostility, even threats and retaliations. One of the hardest things to do in these situations is to keep your cool and avoid aggressive behaviour in response. I have found, however, that condescending silence can be just as destructive as responding angrily, as any agreements reached are usually broken or ignored later on. Sometimes, a little confrontation is useful to reveal hidden agendas or concerns.

To ensure the most favourable outcome in these situations you should consider the following actions:

- **Prepare for difficult situations by building your negotiating power.** Improve your power of threat, trade or relationship. Strengthen your BATNA.

- **Don't become defensive.** Listen carefully to what they are saying and ask questions to clarify. Ask the question, "How do you suggest we solve this?" Listen to what they propose *without* commitment.

- **You may need to take a "time out".** This break may be mental or physical. I have had to excuse myself for a "bathroom break" in order to compose myself and avoid making an antagonistic response to a hostile party. If this is not possible, take a mental check. As clichéd as it sounds, counting to ten may not be a bad idea to give you the time you need.

- **Consider whether you might be provoking their behaviour.** You may not be aware that something you have said or done has aggravated the situation. Apologise if necessary and check your own behaviour.

- **Discover why they are behaving that way.** Many times, individuals do not intend to be difficult but are dealing with underlying circumstances that are influencing their conduct. Early in my career as a medical representative, I visited a doctor who was very aggressive to me for no apparent reason. He actually tossed my products out of his office window. With some further questioning, I discovered that he was upset because he was robbed the week before by someone posing as a medical representative, and he felt that my manager should have introduced me. He then apologised for his behaviour and eventually became one of my best clients.

- **Work on simple issues first**. If a single issue is stalling or becoming contentious, you may want to put it aside and agree on simpler issues first before returning to it.

- **Reframe the issue if possible**. Sometimes, looking at an issue from a different angle brings a new perspective to the situation. I was part of a group that sought corporate sponsorship for events. Our events were designed for six hundred people, a number far less than most companies were prepared to support. However, we were very successful in raising the necessary funds by reframing the description of our audience as "innovators" in the market, who would be early adopters of new products and become advocates to the general population.

- **Present multiple options**. Very often, a difficult negotiator refuses to share any information with you. Proposals can be used to gain information. Present them with multiple options and say, "I know that you will probably not like any of these proposals but I'm asking you to look at them and tell me which one you hate the least." Their response will give you a fair indication of their underlying interests.

- **Consider making a low-value concession as a first move**. This is sometimes necessary to get stalled talks moving. Make sure that the other party understands that the concession is being traded for their full cooperation. You should also offer a concession that has relatively low-value to you, but is valued by the other side.

- **Change the negotiation process**. You may be having a difficult time because of the format of the negotiation. I have resolved many difficult telephone negotiations by meeting the other party in person. Consider whether changing the process will bring a better result.

- **Accept disproportionate responsibility.** If you decide that reaching agreement is to your benefit, accept a disproportionate responsibility to find solutions. Ignore the fact that you are putting in an unfair amount of effort to solve their problems as well.

Spirus developed a comprehensive approach to dealing with Rukor's aggression. He was prepared for Rukor's insults and never responded in kind. He also changed the process of the negotiation by introducing the scroll at a time when Rukor was demanding an immediate surrender. Yoshi's timing of the Greek fire communicated clearly that Cyden was in a position of strength.

Anthos knew that Rukor would not volunteer any information to his father, so he embedded multiple interests into the "prophecy" then measured Rukor's response to them. This helped Spirus to reframe the conversation around power, rather than on food or weapons. Anthos also created the solutions for Apa's plight as he understood that although Rukor would benefit significantly from his inventions, Cyden would meet its objectives of avoiding war and gaining new metallurgy skills from Jude. His acceptance of this disproportionate responsibility was critical to the avoidance of war and the negotiation's mutually beneficial outcome.

9.

Prepare, prepare, prepare

What accounted more than anything else for Spirus' success in this negotiation?

That's right! Preparation.

People generally under-prepare for negotiations, regardless of the stakes. However, planning and preparation are the keys to reaching a successful outcome. An analysis is required not only of your own situation, but of the other party's as well. The following planning checklist can guide you through this process:

☑ What are your goals? Can they be defined by concrete, measurable terms such as dollar amounts? Are you aiming high enough? Do you have enough room for making concessions?

☑ What are *their* goals?

☑ Prioritise your goals. Which are most important? What are you prepared to concede to meet your key objectives? What concessions will you ask for in return? Consider the other side's priorities as well.

☑ What are the interests behind your goals? What are the needs, concerns, desires or fears behind your goals?

☑ What do you think are *their* underlying interests?

☑ What is your BATNA? Let this determine your walk away point. You should never accept an agreement that is not as good as your best alternative. Can you improve your BATNA?

☑ What is their BATNA? If you can figure out their best alternative, then you can offer them *just* a bit more. Can you raise doubts in their mind about their BATNA?

☑ Where does the balance of power lie? Can you improve your powers of threat or trade? Can you neutralise theirs? Is the relationship between the parties strong? Is it important?

☑ Which tactics or tricks are they likely to use? How will you deal with them?

☑ What resistance do you anticipate? How will you overcome it?

☑ Is there anything about the situation that you can change in your favour, such as deadlines, location, composition of the negotiating teams, rules or regulations?

☑ Does the other party have the appropriate authority to make firm commitments to agreements? Do you? Who else do you need to involve?

☑ What questions can you ask to encourage the other side to share information about their needs? How will you get them to open up to you?

☑ What options can you think of that will bring mutual gain? How much information are you willing to share? Are there other parties who can help brainstorm fresh ideas?

☑ Are there any objective standards that you should refer to in the negotiation? Will a neutral third-party add value to the process? Are third-party testimonials appropriate?

☑ How likely is an agreement to stand? How can any implementation problems be avoided or overcome?

10.

Agreement

How could Spirus be comfortable that his agreement with Rukor would be honoured?

No agreement has any worth unless it is honoured after the negotiation is complete. In many instances, an agreement can fall apart when parties have not properly examined how it will be implemented. Other times, it may be necessary to get buy-in from constituents who were not part of the negotiations and may not agree with the decisions made. Even in simple cases, negotiators may experience "the winner's curse" which refers to the discomfort they may feel if a deal is settled too easily. They may ask, "Could I have held out for a higher price?" or "Is there something wrong with this product? Why did I get such a good deal?"

Another condition that influences a high number of returns to retail outlets is "buyer's remorse", or the sense of regret that consumers feel after making a large purchase. This can come from their discussions with family and friends, continuing to comparison shop *after* they have already completed the sale, or their own doubts or lack of confidence in their decision. Buyers should try to minimise the effects of buyer's remorse by gathering as much information as possible *before* making the purchase. Sellers should also be familiar with this phenomenon and develop strategies to reduce it by implementing a good follow-up programme to reinforce the buyer's decision to purchase. Even a simple "thank you" card can help, especially if it's handwritten.

Parties also need to account for cultural differences in the way agreements are written. For example, when I accepted a senior position at a financial company with a very formal culture, I was presented with a detailed, multi-paged contract that specifically outlined every possible circumstance or eventuality. Later on in my career as a marketer, I moved to Jamaica to work for a company with a very different culture; one that placed a high value on relationships and trust. I prepared to receive the contract from my new employer with my legal advisor on hand, only to discover that my contract was a simple letter in the form of a general agreement. In that instance, the organisation expected that parties would look to the relationship to resolve issues, rather than the details of the contract. Similar differences exist between nationalities as well. British negotiators, for example, expect a much more specific agreement than their Indian or Chinese counterparts.

In the global business environment, successful negotiators recognise that negotiation is a continuous process and not just a one-time event ending with the signing of an agreement. One estimate suggests that over eighty percent of business transactions are governed by contractual agreements that have become significantly more complex, with complicated legal terms and conditions governing a myriad of issues. Parties run the risk of assuming that negotiations are over when the deal is signed, and do not realise that the negotiation is only final when the implementation is completed. Parties may also have different perspectives on their respective responsibilities. Agreements need to be monitored and renegotiated as necessary. Parties can agree to review periodically, or only if one side fails to live up to its obligations.

Spirus was able to negotiate out of harm's way, but agreements need to be *implemented* in order to be successful. Anthos needed to ensure that his ideas were properly put into operation, while Havark had to prepare a stronger army to effectively discourage any future aggression. Spirus would also have to improve diplomatic relations with Rukor in order to ensure the longevity of the negotiated agreement they had in place.

·RECOMMENDED READING·

Alder, N. J., (1997). *International Dimensions of Organizational Behaviour.* Cincinnati, Ohio: South-Western College Publishing

Cohen, H. (1980). *You Can Negotiate Anything.* NJ; Lyle Stuart

Dawson, R. (1999). *Secrets of Power Negotiating for Salespeople: Inside Secrets from a Master Negotiator.* NJ: The Career Press.

Fisher, R., & Ertel, D. (1995). *Getting Ready to Negotiate: The Getting to Yes Workbook.* New York: Penguin

Fisher, R.,Ury, W., & Patton, B. (1991). *Getting to Yes: Negotiating Agreement Without Giving In (2nd ed).* New York: Penguin

Karass, G. (1985). *Negotiate to Close: How to Make More Successful Deals.* New York: Simon & Schuster.

Lewicki, R., Saunders, D., Barry, B., & Minton, J. (1997). *Essentials of Negotiation.* New York: McGraw-Hill

Raffia, H. (1982). *The Art and Science of Negotiation.* Cambridge, MA: Belknap Press of Harvard University Press

Shell, G. R. (2000). *Bargaining for Advantage: Negotiation Strategies for Reasonable People.* New York: Penguin

Smith, H. (1988). *Selling Through Negotiation: The Handbook of Sales Negotiation.* New York: AMACOM

Susskind, L., McKearnan, S., & Thomas-Larmer, J (1999). *The Consensus Building Handbook.* Thousand Oaks, CA: Sage Publications

Ury, W. (1991). *Getting Past No: Negotiating with Difficult People.* New York: Bantam Books

Wheeler, M. (2000). *Teaching Negotiation: Ideas and Innovations.* Cambridge, MA: Program on Negotiation at Harvard Law School

·About the Author·

André Bello is an independent consultant in the Caribbean, originally from Trinidad & Tobago, now resident in Jamaica. He is the author of the book "The Sword & the Spirit." This teaching tool was written to simplify core negotiation principles, towards a better understanding of the subject by a mainstream audience. He has enjoyed a progressive career in sales, advertising and marketing since 1990, and wrote his book after completing the program on "Teaching Negotiation in the Organisation" at the Program on Negotiation at Harvard Law School.

Initially a natural scientist, André developed a passion for negotiation theory while completing his MBA. His marketing foundation was deeply grounded in sales as a medical representative for Novartis. In his opinion, there is no substitute for a sales background to truly develop an appreciation for the role of relationships in business. His career path then took him towards advertising at Lonsdale Saatchi & Saatchi, where after only a few months, he played an integral role in winning several new accounts and was made Account Director for PepsiCo International. Based on his success at Lonsdale, one of his key Clients invited him to create a new marketing department for their group of financial companies.

As General Manager of Marketing for the Maritime Financial Group, André worked on the development of client-centric strategies for insurance and investment products. He focused on brand building and lead-generation activities to support personal selling by field agents, and implemented several initiatives that offered value-added benefits to insurance holders. He then migrated to Jamaica, with his wife Frances, to accept the challenge of repositioning an international investment brokerage company, Jamaica Money Market Brokers (JMMB) from its product-centric orientation to a more relationship-centric model. This comprehensive program involved a total re-engineering of JMMB's corporate communications and brand identity, as well as the development of response-based direct marketing tactics. His portfolio also included Sales, New Product Development and Channel Management, and he served as part of the executive team responsible for crafting the strategic direction of the organisation. As a newcomer to the Jamaican business community, André ensured he was properly introduced by founding the organization Boom Networking, an innovative networking fraternity for Caribbean business professionals.

André has recently retired from his executive management position with JMMB, to pursue a full-time consultancy career, specialising in creating client-centric corporate transformations. His focus is mainly in negotiation skills and consultative selling. In addition, he represents professional development programs from the Service Quality Institute, a global leader in customer service. He is a popular speaker and corporate trainer, and delivers in-house seminars for Caribbean companies. In November 2005, he was invited to Paris to present his paper, "The Muscles of Imagination: The Role of Storytelling in Negotiation Training." This international conference on "New Trends in Negotiation Training" was held by Harvard Law School's Program on Negotiation and ESSEC's Institute for Research and Education on Negotiation in Europe, and attracted some of the leading thinkers in the field. André is quickly gaining a reputation as an international speaker in Negotiation Skills.

You can learn more about André and the exciting field of negotiation at **www.andrebello.com**.

·ORDERING ADDITIONAL BOOKS·

Please see our on-line store at www.kiwipublishing.com for a complete listing of all André Bello related products.

· Telephone orders: Toll Free from the US - 1.866.836.7913
· Web orders: www.kiwipublishing.com
· Postal orders: KIWI PUBLISHING, INC.,
                    P.O. Box 3852, Woodbridge,
                    CT 06525-3852

André Bello is available for private speaking engagements, corporate and small business training. Visit Mr. Bello's website at www.andrebello.com

Please contact KIWI Publishing for:
· Other publications, audio cd's
· Consulting services
· National & International Seminars

DON'T MISS THE FIRST ANNUAL NEGOTIATION &
PRODUCTIVITY CONFERENCE
Jamaica, November 2006

Questions? Comments?
Please e-mail us at info@kiwipublishing.com.